GIFTED

8 STEPS TO SUCCEEDING IN SPORT, WORK, AND LIFE

Robert J. Schinke, EdD

Library of Congress Cataloging-in-Publication Data

Names: Schinke, Robert J., author.
Title: Gifted : 8 steps to succeeding in sport, work, and life / Robert J. Schinke, PhD.
Description: Champaign, IL : Human Kinetics, [2025] | Includes bibliographical references.
Identifiers: LCCN 2023055990 (print) | LCCN 2023055991 (ebook) | ISBN 9781718229310 (paperback) | ISBN 9781718229327 (epub) | ISBN 9781718229334 (pdf)
Subjects: LCSH: Positive psychology. | Self-realization. | Ability. | Success. | BISAC: SPORTS & RECREATION / Sports Psychology | HEALTH & FITNESS / Exercise / General
Classification: LCC BF204.6 .S243 2025 (print) | LCC BF204.6 (ebook) | DDC 150.19/88--dc23/eng/20240221
LC record available at https://lccn.loc.gov/2023055990
LC ebook record available at https://lccn.loc.gov/2023055991

ISBN: 978-1-7182-2931-0 (print)

Copyright © 2025 by Robert Schinke

Human Kinetics supports copyright. Copyright fuels scientific and artistic endeavor, encourages authors to create new works, and promotes free speech. Thank you for buying an authorized edition of this work and for complying with copyright laws by not reproducing, scanning, or distributing any part of it in any form without written permission from the publisher. You are supporting authors and allowing Human Kinetics to continue to publish works that increase the knowledge, enhance the performance, and improve the lives of people all over the world.

To report suspected copyright infringement of content published by Human Kinetics, contact us at **permissions@hkusa.com**. To request permission to legally reuse content published by Human Kinetics, please refer to the information at **https://US.HumanKinetics.com/pages/permissions-translations-faqs**.

The web addresses cited in this text were current as of November 2023, unless otherwise noted.

Acquisitions Editor: Diana Vincer; **Managing Editor:** Hannah Werner; **Senior Graphic Designer:** Sean Roosevelt; **Cover Designer:** Keri Evans; **Cover Design Specialist:** Susan Rothermel Allen; **Cover Graphic:** Kykyshka/iStock/Getty Images; **Interior Graphic:** royyimzy/AdobeStock.com; **Photo Production Manager:** Jason Allen; **Production:** Westchester Publishing Services; **Printer:** Cushing-Malloy, Inc.

Human Kinetics books are available at special discounts for bulk purchase. Special editions or book excerpts can also be created to specification. For details, contact the Special Sales Manager at Human Kinetics.

Printed in the United States of America   10 9 8 7 6 5 4 3 2 1

Human Kinetics
1607 N. Market Street
Champaign, IL 61820
USA

United States and International
Website: **US.HumanKinetics.com**
Email: info@hkusa.com
Phone: 1-800-747-4457

Canada
Website: **Canada.HumanKinetics.com**
Email: info@hkcanada.com

E9538

GIFTED

8 STEPS TO SUCCEEDING IN SPORT, WORK, AND LIFE

I dedicate this book and associated hours of writing and sculpting to you, the reader, and your untapped gifts. Human gifts are special—they are at the marrow in each of us. I also wish to express immense gratitude to my immediate family, being my partner Erin, sons Harrison and Pierce, and mother-in-law Kelly, for their encouragement and support in the germinating of creative ideas. Appreciation also goes out to the international colleagues who've helped me better understand the world where we live. These are societal colleagues and members I have met in travels whilst contributing to the International Society of Sport Psychology and the Association for Applied Sport Psychology. Dieter Hackfort, Gangyan Si, Liwei Zhang, Jean Williams, Tara Scanlan, Glyn Roberts, Gershon Tenenbaum, Natalia Stambulova, Ernest Hung, and YoungHo Kim have been immeasurably supportive.

—Robert Schinke

CONTENTS

Introduction ix

The Equestrian — 1

Lesson One: Gifts   5

Lesson Two: Forces   17

Lesson Three: Contortions   33

The Social Scientist — 51

Lesson Four: Glimpses   57

Lesson Five: Endurance   75

The Mental Performance Consultant — 101

Lesson Six: Transcendence   105

Lesson Seven: Symmetry   125

The Educator-Mentor — 141

Lesson Eight: Regifting   147

Conclusion 165 • Glossary 173 • References 179 •
About the Author 187

INTRODUCTION

The world of self-help books includes many options, each proposing its own potential growth opportunity. As you comb through vast columns of books or lists of new releases in search of a suitable self-improvement topic, your health and well-being within sports, work, and play will influence your choice. Several years ago, while on the verge of dropping out of university at a critical time in my doctoral studies, I was drawn to a particular self-improvement book. The crossroad before me was whether to continue in academic studies or transition entirely into the field of applied sport psychology as a **mental performance consultant** (1). A mental performance consultant is someone who supports aspiring performers within the contexts of sports and physical activity as well as in settings such as music, dance, and the military (2). Focus is often placed on one's motivation, career development, and personal growth through **mental skills** (3). In this book, you will explore several of these mental skills, particularly those relating to goals, visualization, performance **planning**, concentration, and especially, self-reflection. You also will learn several terms and their accompanying interventions that are borrowed from motivational theories. The most creditable supportive strategies from applied sport psychology content are infused with up-to-date theory and steeped in scientific testing, but I digress. The book I chose to read and apply was *Learned Optimism: How to Change Your Mind and Your Life* (4). Dr. Martin E. F. Seligman's book was inspirational, founded on scientific knowledge, and written for a practical readership. I wanted to develop my ideas in a similar style by blending research and practice into a systematic approach that would be useful to ambitious athletes, those who supported them, and people wishing to adopt life skills from the world of elite sports. My goal was to help affirm meaning in people's lives, just as Dr. Seligman's book helped me consider my gifts and persist as a scientist practitioner working on the front lines of elite sports (4).

How did you happen upon this book? Your life might have been running along smoothly until a certain point when you lost some footing. Maybe you or someone you know is recovering from a challenging life circumstance. The feeling of being unsettled in one or more facets of life is a common experience. The human condition will always include finding and deviating from your path, something that tends to happen through a combination of intuition, availing possibilities, self-awareness, and correction. You know what life feels like when you are on your right path: your mood is great; you sleep well; and your work, play, and relationships feel harmonious. Your body is also responding well—you have a spring in your step at the start of each day. But sometimes you will feel uncertain, as if the earth beneath your feet is soft and unsettled and you cannot gain traction in your life course. During times of uncertainty, you might become insecure, irritable, frustrated, or sad because you are not getting the most out of yourself and the world around you. This book is written to help explain the differences between being on your best path and being on a path that doesn't feel right and then to help you find healthier, better-aligned alternatives.

When you feel satisfied with life, it is because you are tapping into and drawing upon your gifts throughout each day. This book can become a catalyst, accelerant, or necessary support as you move closer to your best-suited path. No path is perfectly linear. To expect linearity is unreasonable and unrealistic. So, you must be compassionate with yourself and come to appreciate detours for what they offer. There will be unavoidable and unpredictable bumps along the way. You will be tested time and again. Accept the imperfect road before you, but as much as possible, choose to journey in your truest direction.

Who am I to encourage you to move toward your gifts? How is my perspective a useful lens and potential resource on your journey? Some years ago, my athletic career was at an end. As a former equestrian national team member, I was invited by the Canadian Olympic Committee to be an on-site volunteer at a Pan-American Games and at the following year's Olympic Games. Traveling to the events, I met staff and athletes from many sports disciplines. Through the process, I observed the challenges of pursuing athletic gifts and the lived experiences and requests of athletes, coaches, and administrators chasing their dreams. Concurrently, I was immersed in a PhD program and continued to gather basic theoretical and scientific skills in a blend of sport science and psychology. My task as a volunteer at these formative major events was to shuttle technical staff and coaches to their venues each day and then back to their accommodations. Every afternoon, after everyone returned from their events, we met outside the private hotel residence to celebrate another day of collective Olympic experiences over food and drinks. I wanted to work within elite boxing because of its association with grit and determination. I intentionally met the boxing team's leader and brought him his afternoon coffee, which he drank while smoking cigarettes one after another. After several days he became progressively talkative. Sparked by discussions of sports and my relentless questions about the boxing world, we began an enduring friendship, one which lasted to the end of his life. Our friendship opened the world of combative sports to me and with it came an opportunity to work with the Olympians he was overseeing. Before long, I began to accompany the athletes and coaches to training camps and then to major international events, a journey that consumed 25 years.

Within two years of Olympic boxing consulting, I was approached to work with the first of several professional boxing management groups. Word had spread that internationally known amateur athletes liked working and traveling with me and that they were also performing extremely well on the international stage. These athletes desired motivational support, but equally, it was my personal approach and style of delivery that they related to, including my use of language, clothing, and how I navigated the reluctance of less-trusting athletes. After four years with Olympic boxing, I was fully employed with several professional boxing management groups and attended major televised events. At the same time, I was helping international athletes from a wide variety of sports, such as figure skating, badminton, squash, equestrian, tennis, golf, and ice hockey. Within boxing, my **path** culminated in clients achieving success during HBO and Showtime sporting events. Athletes who were once on the brink of success became world champions, filling large sports arenas and securing their futures. I was hired to strengthen working relationships among the athletes and their entourages and became a trusted member of tightly bound teams. I have spent countless days, weeks, months, and years on the road supporting world-class athletes as they chased down their gifts in the sporting arenas and in their broader life ambitions.

I transitioned to full-time mental performance consulting after completing a PhD. Despite working with a full complement of professional athletes, I remained inspired by the book I previously carried from the research lab to my home and back again each day during those two final years of graduate studies. Eager to continue academic learning, I contacted the book's author and was blessed with a one-year postdoctoral opportunity to study with him and his colleague Dr. Christopher Peterson, a social psychologist from the University of Michigan. Our time together was focused on a rapidly growing and high-profile subject area in psychology known as positive psychology. Identifying the potential strengths in people remains the focus in positive psychology, and the area consists of a growing number of topics including resilience, courage, social intelligence, wisdom, justice, and humanity (6). Human resilience was my chosen topic, driven by my experiences as a relentless student, athlete, and young professional. Resilience, with its well-developed literary base (7), was also a recurring point of discussion among my clients. Like my mentors, I wanted to help support positive changes in people through research-informed practice, in my case, partly through resilience training. My mandate was to work on the front lines of world-class sports, taking what I was learning through my research and then providing my clients with cutting-edge services to help strengthen their performance advantage. The idea of writing an inspirational book during these early times in my career was not within the realm of possibility. The idea surfaced and dissipated many times before I eventually steeled myself with encouragement from my partner and wrote this book for you.

In this book, several of the examples are taken from boxing, an intriguing and dramatic sport. Boxers are often born without means and many emigrate from war-torn countries or impoverished circumstances, escaping with their lives and the clothes on their backs. Most begin their journeys penniless and unable to afford a coffee, like the original story of Rocky. Boxing, when performed at the highest level, represents a way out of poverty, limited education, poor living conditions, crime, and the disbelief of naysayers. Boxing brings to life the concept of embracing one's qualities, walking with them to the ring, fighting for what and who one believes in, and enduring the hardships of battle to success at the final bell. The person who endures becomes the victor; the person who relents becomes the conquered. Without the sport of boxing and its myriad stories of inspiration, we would miss the splendid metaphor of how to battle to our version of personal success in everyday life. The most important lesson you can learn from boxing is that at times you will need to steel yourself and fight for what you believe in, particularly the value of your gifts.

This Book and You

You come to this book with your own gifts, uniqueness, personal story, and accumulated experiences. Gifts are aptitudes you bring with you into the world—characteristics that make you, well, you. Your gifts might be in the form of a certain way of thinking, creativity, an artistic talent, athleticism, courageousness, generosity of spirit, kindness, compassion, and more. You were born with several gifts that when used will bring out your very finest and most authentic version of yourself. Gifts come naturally to you, and so they must flow from you like water from a tap. Life should be, as much as possible, about staying in close touch with your innate gifts, their application, and their evolution. Much like whiskey, wine, and other fine commodities, your gifts must be released from anything holding them back, they must be given freedom to develop, and their fine qualities must be enjoyed. Sadly, not all people choose to discover who they really are. Many of those who do are inconsistent in honing their skills and sharing them with the world around. By choosing not to develop one's gifts, people unwisely withhold parts of themselves or their entire personhood. They pass up opportunities to develop their gifts to full potential in many creative enterprises. Why are your gifts so important to you and the world you live in? Imagine a world where every person withheld their natural gifts. Creativity would stagnate, and important discoveries that could benefit all people and our planet would decrease. There would be no cures for disease, no scientific approaches to inspire people, and no creative genius of any sort. The world would be a muted place to live; you and I would go about our day without vigor, placing one foot in front of the other with no vision and no meaning.

This book is about a series of recurring discussions presented as eight themed **lessons**, each its own crossroad, necessitating wise choices. I gathered these lessons having lived as an athlete, elite coach, and a mental performance consultant. My professional career has been devoted to working with world-class athletes before and at the crest of Olympic and professional sports events, as well as with people in disciplines outside of sports, such as education and business. This book was written to support you as you seek to be your most gifted self each day. When you prepare and then perform as you are meant to, drawing upon your unique skills and talents in each part of daily life, only then is your version of excellence possible. Your forward movement toward achieving excellence can only be secured by tapping into these gifts, by being your unique self each day, by relishing the moments when you are living how you are meant to live, by testing your resolve, and by enduring relentlessly until you move day by day beyond earlier performance levels. Then you can apply what you have learned in one area of life across daily activities. You can pass on the lessons you have learned in terms of cultivating personal gifts to the people around you so they can flourish too.

Being you—and others being their true gifted selves—will not always be easy, given the world we live in. You have daily commitments, demands, and expectations to tackle. These demands will bring internal and external forces to the forefront and encourage your move toward or away from your gifts. Demands on your time sometimes will not align with your personal gifts. You may have to choose between being who you are and sticking to your values or changing into some other version of yourself that feels unnatural, uncomfortable, foreign, confining, and unpleasant. Allow this book to become a source of support to you on an **authentic** path. There is a distinct difference between going through the motions of your life performance and being engaged, intuitive, innovative, and only then, becoming your version of world class.

Scope and Content of This Book

The eight curated developmental lessons have each been assigned a keyword meant to reveal its simplest form. Each keyword presents its own important teaching, signifies a decisional crossroad, and is crafted to guide you onto the path you desire and deserve by your **birthright**. Although the lessons are presented in sequence, we don't move through life in a linear path, from one lesson to the next, with the earlier lesson already mastered and evident. You will sometimes need to return to each lesson at a more suitable time to ensure you stay on a healthy path and to recognize when you might be taking a path not authentically best for you. The developmental lessons derived at monumental crossroads in your life are as follows:

1. Remembrance of your natural **gifts**
2. **Forces** that can pull you toward and away from these gifts
3. Potential response of changing shape, or **contortion**
4. Recurring **glimpses** of your gifts and reminders of how these can reinvigorate you providing you stop for a moment to recognize them
5. **Endurance** when you begin to use your gifts to overcome life's challenges
6. Moments of **transcendence** when you deliver excellence by strategically tapping into your gifts in crucial settings
7. **Symmetries**, meaning applying your gifts in as many areas of life as you dare to develop a well-blended strategy that carries across your days and weeks
8. **Regifting**, in which you encourage the exploration and application of giftedness in other people, and in so doing, reinforce your own gift as an experienced traveler on your path of giftedness

Throughout these eight lessons, unnamed examples are provided, in which high-level performers—athletes, coaches, educators, and people from the service industry—often make wise decisions and choose to pursue excellence in their lives by using well-developed tradecraft.

The term *tradecraft* alludes to the tricks of the trade that spies use to carry out their surreptitious missions. High-level performers, coaches, and mission staff are no different from spies in the way they approach their training and competitions. Every aspect of their training environment is crafted to foster performance. This is very much their own form of tradecraft. No two athletes are alike in how they prepare, nor are they alike in their tradecraft. Thus, in writing this book I had to find the balance between illuminating athlete tradecraft without divulging a telltale detail that might expose the athlete's training secrets. As athletes come closer to their performance date, their circle of support reflects the myopic focus of performance by becoming narrower and eliminating any chance of their preparation being made public. Closed-door training sessions: meetings that are in-person only, thereby eliminating the chance of emails being circulated outside of the inner team; and hunkering down at a training base off the beaten path are all means to protect their trade. Although the athlete-related experiences and corresponding learning points shared within this book had their genesis in these very protected environments, naming the athletes themselves is simply not possible.

Progressive **stories** from my developmental process are layered into this book. These stories are placed where they make sense as examples of a treasured gift. In place of my stories, **reflect** and layer in your own stories as you recognize and curate your own amazing gifts. The stories are used to illustrate the discovering, rediscovering, and transferring of gifts from one time or part of your life into another over a progressive and rewarding journey. Stories are powerful **affirmation** tools you will eventually be asked to use as you reflect on where you began and affirm the strengths you have used along the way in building the best version of yourself. The stories might represent snapshots in time when you were most on track and content with your life, or they may represent times when you discovered a jolting life lesson that was critical in your evolution.

Each lesson includes one or more action items, followed by a review list with four key reminders to help you remember and refine your reinvigorated or newfound skills. To reinforce language and understanding, a glossary directly follows the concluding chapter. Each term will be in bold font when first used to identify its inclusion in the glossary. Scientific publications, a variety of websites, and a few documentaries are cited sparingly but are included in a reference list at the end of the book if you wish to follow up and look deeper into a topic. Each reference is marked by a chronological number, often placed at the end of the sentence where the idea is found. So, you could read the book from front to back without drawing on the supplemental material, which is perfectly fine, or you may prefer to access the supplemental scientific resources as you read this book. You have a style of learning—let your reading strategy dictate.

Finally, there is one main message throughout this book: If you recognize and believe in your natural gifts and uniqueness, you must stand your ground. Whether the forces upon you are personal or social, you must persist to reveal excellence across all parts of your life. You are, and will always be, a work in progress. Life lessons are learned continually, and each lesson adds to the depth of your gifts and your enjoyment of them.

Consider this fact: There exists in you a sizable and brilliant potential, in which your gifts are pursued and they are also boundless. Excellence is your birthright—something you began with and now must polish to a luster. All you need is a little insight and the means and encouragement to carry out the journey ahead. This book is crafted to help you develop your most desired gifts when you choose to tap into them.

THE EQUESTRIAN

A wise horseman earned most of his living buying and selling horses. He provided income for his young family. Each spring, he would contact a local horse breeder and bring in talented youngstock from the animals he looked over in the breeder's field. The selected youngstock would arrive at his stable, practically untouched and wary of human hands. The horseman had a son, his protégé. He and his son would work with the horses one by one, handling them, grooming them, and often backing them—meaning placing bridle and saddle and then sitting on each one so the horses could be ridden by potential buyers in waiting.

One spring, a nervous, wiry, and unpredictable horse stood out from the others. When she moved, she floated effortlessly across the ground. However, what separated her from the other youngstock was her tendency to jump from one field to the next as she galloped ungoverned across the horseman's property. In her mind, this was her rightful domain regardless of fencing and the confinement of the other horses. She explored the property each day, bounding from field to field, much to the curiosity and delight of the horseman. This horse was magnificent and quite different from the others.

One day a well-regarded international equestrian traveled from out of the country to purchase the horse based on her breeding lineage. The buyer was interested in the horse only for her movement and intended to train the horse to fulltime dressage, an equestrian discipline akin to dancing. The horseman was sad to see this horse go, but he could not explain away his sadness and loss in that moment other than to justify it as his role to sell youngstock and support his family. She was loaded into a trailer and the horseman watched the trailer fade into the distance from the top of his driveway as she was taken to her new home. The horse stayed at her new lodging from the age of two until the age of three, one spring later. Over the course of that year, she became progressively unhappy and uncooperative with the tasks she was expected to perform as her life's work.

The horseman received an unexpected phone call from the equestrian the following spring, asking whether the magnificent horse could be returned and exchanged for a less spirited animal, one who would accept the art of dressage as its life's work. Sensing the opportunity before him, the horseman immediately agreed to the exchange. One week later, the magnificent horse was returned. The horseman again stood at the top of the driveway, this time as the trailer and former buyer returned. The horse, she explained, could not be properly broken. The term *broken* has often been used by some horse trainers to mark the moment a human sits on a horse and rides it with bridle and saddle. The term also holds a symbolic meaning, implying the bending of spirit and personality to the will of another. Some horse people believe their job is to shape a horse's will to their human vision and desire. The horse is then re-created into something often unrecognizable from its original birthright and tendencies. This concept of breaking—forcing one into formulaic or conventional pathways to avoid difficulty, challenge, or hardship—is familiar across all living beings.

The horse was quickly off-loaded and handed back to the horseman, who in turn handed off the horse to his protégé son. Before the buyer and seller walked to the horseman's home to share a pot of coffee, sign paperwork, and embark on their trade of horses, he whispered in his son's ear in the quietest of voice, "This here horse is now yours." Horse and protégé gazed at each other, both uncertain and sizing up one another. The horse knew exactly who she was—a free, untamed, and unyielding spirit. The young man was a promising equestrian with an interest in three-day eventing, a sport combining the disciplines of dressage, cross-country, and show jumping, interests compatible with his new horse. He too was a solitary being often engaged in his own activities.

Horse and rider seemed to recognize a little of themselves in the life standing before them. Within weeks they embarked on a journey that personified who they were, not as separate entities, but as a unified expression. They were the perfect blend of spirit, uniqueness, resilience, and vision. Together they galloped across the horseman's fields, leaping over fences with abandon and shared joy. The horse didn't mind having a partner in her adventures, and the rider shared in a sense of abandon not yet experienced on any previous horses. Before long, the two individuals melded into a partnership, each learning and compounding the adventurous spirit of the other. Within a much shorter time than typically needed for horse and rider to progress, they became world-class competitors, despite their shared youth and inexperience.

The horse was named Solitaire on the day of her reacquisition and handing over to the young man, a name that aligned with her character. One meaning for the word *solitaire* is a perfectly cut, authentic, priceless diamond. We are each a solitaire by birthright and hold the potential of refinement into our version of the extraordinary. A second meaning is that of an entity standing apart from those around it, with distance self- or externally imposed.

This story an abbreviated but true lived experience. The true story is also a metaphor. Significance is found in the horse's will to forge her own path forward despite initial counterweighted human will. You will also experience times when you are asked to set aside your gifts and become something ordinary or foreign. Yet you must recognize and embrace, as both horse and rider did, your deeply rooted talents and abilities. These gifts are rightfully yours and should never be surrendered or disregarded because they affirm who you truly are.

LESSON ONE
GIFTS

> *Life is not easy for any of us. But what of that? We must have perseverance and above all confidence in ourselves. We must believe that we are gifted for something, and that this thing must be attained.*
>
> Marie Curie

You were born with a vast pool of gifts and talents that cannot be evaluated based only on one moment in time. Gifts are abilities you can easily turn your hand to when you so choose, just as they are wonderful qualities you could encourage in people you meet. Examples of sport gifts are athletic speed, endurance, strength, agility, or tactical IQ. Nonsport gifts include making a strong argument, crafting words into stories, business savvy, and engaging others in learning. Gifts are a necessary part of your healthy existence in a flourishing life. It is humane and kind to tap into your gifts, and it is inhumane and uncaring to ignore them in yourself or another person. Exceptional abilities—yours, and those of family, friends, colleagues, or protégés—can either be recognized, tapped, and polished, or they can be unrecognized, untouched, discouraged, and underdeveloped to the point where they become much like an atrophied muscle.

What does it take to become the very best version of who you are by birthright? The answer, at least in part, requires a willingness, regardless of life's daily challenges, to be several parts of your true self in place of one. For example, a work-related gift that aligns with a recreational pursuit can be brought into your home and shared with family and friends. You must be authentically you in terms of the visibility and application of your gifts, talents, and personality. Despite the uniqueness coded into each of us, it is common to have our individuality, including our gifts, questioned throughout our lives. We must often choose between holding tightly to who we are or relenting to life pressures and becoming someone we no longer recognize. We are tested time and again as we reach for our gifts, but the outcomes from these tests vary with each person. As I will share throughout this book, we sometimes stay the course and play to our gifts, using these as we are meant to. Think back to the activities you loved as a child. The sorts of gifts that spring to your mind are not important, but your passion for them is mission critical. Take two minutes over a sip of tea or coffee and think back to a unique gift you discovered about yourself in childhood. When your memory is revisited even now, chances are it brings a twinkle to your eye and smile to your face. In other instances, you might have dismissed or overlooked one or more of your natural gifts, maybe from a young age or perhaps as an adult. In the process of loss, you have wandered off your optimal pathway and away from your callings and your inspirations. The outcome will inevitably be a feeling shared by many people—that of being a compromised, inhibited, and lesser version of yourself.

Discovering Your Gifts

My first recollection of being profoundly tested in terms of personal gifts was experienced outside my household. Household environments are not exempt from spurring questions of who we are and who we should be, but my giftedness as a learner was tested continually at different developmental times in educational settings from kindergarten until I graduated university and became a professional. The process began when teachers labeled me as "different" upon entry to kindergarten. The entry into the school system the world over is a vulnerable time for children as they continue to learn and develop their sense of self and learn what is acceptable and what isn't. My teacher did not care for me from day one. In her eyes I was different from my classmates and not in a way she liked. I said little, and when I did speak, pronunciation was a challenge. Given my quietness, my first teacher called me a daydreamer, with a look of disapproval, often refusing to acknowledge my presence. I sensed something in her expressions and demeanor—agitation caused by acquiring an unwanted and perhaps ungifted student, likely one among many to that point in her life.

That first year of elementary school shook me to the core, as it does many young children starting out in their educational pursuits. Kindergarten was a first lesson that I would not always be desirable in the eyes of those in my surrounding world, just as you might have experienced some similar feedback early on. Partway through the year, I was sent to a renowned psychiatrist at the request of my teacher and assessed for what she believed to be inevitable learning challenges. I remember sitting with a kind man, playing with puzzles and games, speaking to him, and then being sent into a room to await judgment. What I came to learn was he found me to be well adjusted. The psychiatrist believed I daydreamed because I was not being mentally stimulated and my mind wandered to more accepting places than the uncaring classroom to which I was confined. Upon my return from professional testing, with a positive written evaluation rendered, the teacher reconfigured her approach and tolerance of at least one student. I am still a dreamer—a person who identifies and chases down possibilities in unlikely places by asking unlikely questions. Daydreaming was regarded as a liability in an environment focused on generic school content and rote learning. However, dreaming can be a gift: the place where tremendous opportunities ignite and are then defined, pursued, and captured. Dreams can lead to unconventional thinking about a common problem, inspire geographic exploration, spur the creation of cures for illness, potentially solve global warming, and in my world, dreams can inspire people to excel on high-level stages. However important dreams are, they can only warm over time into the manifestation of gifts when the dreamers and their dreams are nurtured in soft, fertile soil.

To this day, I am unclear what determines the more-gifted versus less-gifted student when listening to educators evaluate aptitude in the students they are meant to help guide. The discussions that sometimes ensue suggest such educators can discern—much like a high-quality coffee, craft beer, wine, or whiskey—suitable from unsuitable students and top-shelf students from middle- and bottom-shelf candidates. These snapshot assessments are founded on personal experiences; they are highly preferential, human, and open to grave mistake, leaving many a vulnerable learner with an externally imposed message of compromised worth, one which can endure for a long time, perhaps indefinitely, depending on how it is interpreted and responded to (8). The experience of being challenged in terms of one's gifts applies to all stages of a lifetime and is shared by all people. The consequence of poor external evaluations, when coupled with weakened self-worth, can lead to a shrinking world with a smaller scope of professional and personal life choices. The person who might have been a gifted educator may opt out of pursuing education altogether, just as the promising athlete might withdraw from sports and look elsewhere, forgoing tremendous talent and joy.

In achievement settings such as professional sports, scouts and coaches judge and misjudge the athletes before them, either securing the diamond in the rough or missing out on tremendous talents and opportunities. Sometimes a gifted athlete's talent is initially overlooked and tapped later, or sometimes the talent is squandered as the athlete continues unnoticed. Some athletes, like some students, are trapped in a system where there is little room for their version of uniqueness, despite its high quality. Recently, one of my sons has taken a liking to a rookie athlete in a popular televised sport. The athlete was drafted several years earlier and sent to a minor league team to develop or languish, depending on current interpretations found in the media. The player was eventually called up to the big leagues, and in the first season, he was among the leading players in the sport, as if emerging out of nowhere. The athlete promptly renegotiated a playing contract in the postseason that happily has led to a well-deserved, sizable, and life-altering salary. Reviewing the athlete's well-documented career path, he is and always has been a standout performer. Human error caused by laziness, an overly narrow understanding of what greatness is, and perhaps an arbitrary dislike of the person contribute to overlooking human gifts and is commonplace. Although you cannot control all the human casualties suffering from oversight, when it comes to yourself and those you touch, there are many opportunities to nurture individual gifts. Furthermore, because you hold a few gifts of your own, your commitment to yourself must be to ensure you rise to your potential each day and play to (and with) your strengths. Gifts are meant to be used and enjoyed.

High school, in my case, was a continuation of what I experienced in elementary school. Certain teachers found me to be talented and able. Their antithesis was an educator who attempted to dispel and nullify the gifts of many students, much as naysayers in your life might have suggested an alternate, less beneficial pathway to you. This antithetical teacher told me and some of my classmates during our final year of secondary school that we were not university material. The final year of high school is an uncertain time for students as they prepare for the life transition from secondary school to a trade, college, or university pursuit. What were the teacher's evaluation criteria for determining who among the students should continue in school and who should find another life path?

I have come to believe in small world theory. We live in a very small world where life often comes full circle if we are paying attention and where truth is ultimately revealed and wrongs can be righted. Some years later, the very same disapproving teacher was safely installed in a faculty position at a university. She had gained her dream position as an academic and educator of bright minds in a higher learning environment. We met by coincidence. I was immersed in graduate studies at the university where she was working, having just ended an athletic career culminating in national team status. This professor wondered what I was doing walking the halls of her department in the university. She seemed physically smaller than I remembered as we faced one another awkwardly. By her expression, she was puzzled and perhaps a little fearful of what was unfolding. I was undertaking a master's degree with distinction, seeking entry into a doctoral program. A PhD was something the educator held dearly as a prized possession reserved for the chosen few. The title "PhD" was one she had referred to in relation to herself as a member of an exclusive club. In secondary school she would often write the acronym PhD on the chalkboard to emphasize her place in the world, underlining the letters as loudly as she possibly could, pressing chalk against chalkboard for further emphasis. When we met as adults, she seemed to be pondering how she could have been so off the mark in terms of the aptitude of the confident person before her. To this day, I am uncertain whether her reaction was because she recognized how she had wronged another person or whether she dismissed me as evidence of the devaluing of higher learning to a business model in which anyone could gain a desired degree with money, time, and endurance. It was likely the latter interpretation, which tends to dispel accountability and the associated shame or guilt of having wronged another person.

Reflecting on Your Discovery Process

Reflecting over the years of my schooling, it has become clearer that encountering naysayers is unavoidable and even necessary to personal growth. The idea that negative judgments should be the end of your gift pursuit is a flawed conclusion. You and I *do* need to harden, meaning we need to strengthen our resolve and build thick, semipermeable skins to buffer against inevitable adversity. This lesson was reinforced to me through a doctoral research project I supervised in partnership with my local medical school (9). The third-year medical students went through a formal hardening process that included self-questioning and harsh critiques from experienced physicians and specialists, which was counterbalanced by moments when their capacity to become physicians was reinforced. The point is that you should recognize your qualities regardless of potentially harmful external influencers you will inevitably meet along the way. In lesson two, I will return to this point about forces and counterforces. We need moments when we are in harmony and moments when we are in disharmony. The tension from these forces teaches you about yourself, your preferences, and ideally, the choices you must move toward and persist with to travel on your authentic path.

Reflect on a time in your life when you were told in no uncertain terms that you were not going to make the grade and that you didn't have the requisite talent to continue your chosen path. How did you feel when the disappointing external judgment was rendered? Were you jolted into a reality in which you chose to discontinue your preferred path, or did you respond with increased resistance to the message and further your energy investment? There is no avoiding negative judgments; we each have met and will continue to meet people and circumstances resistant of our gifts. Ask any athlete, top-notch scientist, or entrepreneur whether someone or something along the way suggested they were not armed for success in the field they now lead. What differentiates those who advance to any apex is a determined attitude to prove oneself or those in the surrounding environment incorrect.

I recently watched an interview with former National Hockey League great Phil Esposito, known for his exceptionally high scoring with the Boston Bruins. As a child he was cut from his local hockey team. Not only was he angered in that moment for having to sit out and watch lesser athletes progress onto the team before being dismissed from its composition, he scolded the coach for consuming the hour of his time leading to the incorrect external judgment (10). He, like others who have defied odds and succeeded at the highest level, refused to take no for an answer. Denial by others is merely a challenge meant to harden you; it's not meant to be the end of any dream and treasured gift. Your chosen path forward and your success need to be determined by you, and the gifts you know are within your grasp. All else is put in place to test and strengthen your resolve and to fortify your commitment.

My own experience as a student continued with several graduate degrees. The formal education process—with its logical conclusion of a doctorate, postdoctoral studies, and what has followed since—has been riddled with bumps, potholes, detours, and barriers that I continue to learn from and overcome. There are always obstacles to be overcome. Like you, I need to tackle each unique challenge, as unpleasant as it might be in the moment, when it is being experienced. From these lessons, this person, once merely a vision in my mind's eye, now exists as a multi-society international leader in the field of sport psychology (11). From where I now stand, there are new and exciting ventures on the horizon in relation to career and personal interests and opportunities for sharing these with my family, friends, and colleagues. Seeking your gifts and opportunities is a necessary condition to a thriving existence. There are always new skills to learn, new people to meet, new scientific questions to explore, and newly discovered gifts to embrace and relish. Similarly, if someone asked you what you were meant to do with your life and who you were meant to be in the finite time you have on this earth, there is an answer you know to be true. So, continue to dream and then to act upon your dreams, substantiating and expanding your vision. You have endless gifts that must give rise to big possibilities, big realities, and big legacies. The question is: How are you to draw upon who you are at best in everything you do each day? This book was written to target your knowledge and intuition and to fortify your internal compass so you are equipped to rally against external pressures and judgments, all while fostering your gifts. Drawing upon lesson one, think about some of the innate gifts you've seen in yourself since childhood. Recognize your wonderful gifts daily and appreciate them as part of the very best version of you. Your first task is to embrace your gifts by writing about them, reinforcing exactly what makes you great.

Lesson One: Gifts | 13

Action Item One: Identifying Your Gifts

Tap into your extraordinary gifts as often as you can every day. Your gifts extend beyond a single environment, such as your work or personal life. Every gift you hold, whether ingenuity, artistry, athleticism, critical thinking, or another talent, is a transferable skill you can bring to every minute of every day. In the world of science, researchers often ask whether skills or findings are transferable across environments, from one to another. With athletes, part of the responsibility of a motivational consultant is to encourage a transferability of skills so each performer is prepared to move from the junior ranks to the senior ranks, from the senior ranks to the world stage, and from the world stage to the next part of their lives—whether as students, business professionals, physicians, musicians, or wherever they journey in their road map to a fulfilling life. When I retired from being an athlete, my gifts were two. First, I always saw problems and their solutions in a different way than many of my contemporaries. Where people attempted to solve problems through conventional scientific theories and approaches that many others before them drew upon, I often considered unconventional approaches, such as those I would generate with my participants and clients beyond the university's walls and conventions. Second, I was also resilient and able to shake off the discouraging words of naysayers. I had spent a childhood, youth, and young adulthood in school settings, playing sports and learning to be a social scientist, in other words, following my own path. I understood, based on the journey, the consequences of morphing into someone else's version of person, athlete, and professional. Those possibilities were not for me. Your gifts are equally unique and transferable, and you are entitled to reach for them without explanation or apology. Your future is yours to forge, and its bounty is yours to harvest.

For the first step in this exercise, reflect upon your childhood and youth. First, find a quiet place where you will be uninterrupted. Stretch out and move until you are in a comfortable position, either reclining or lying down. Then begin rhythmic breathing, much as athletes would at the beginning of a mental warm-up before beginning their physical warm-up and much as you would before drifting off to sleep. Once you have established a good, deep, rhythmic breathing pattern, where your lungs are drawing full breaths of air, journey back using your memory bank to recall memories of your childhood and youth when you first noticed your special personal gift. My best friend (my wife) loved to draw. To this day she can draw with a flowing, light hand. She conjures up a perfect medley of colors in her drawings until they meld into beautiful artistry. My sibling was a creative writer. She could write poetry in primary school that I envy to this day. My grandmother was a chef the likes of which I can only recall from my early childhood. She could create organic custards, ice creams, cured meats, and all sorts of delights. I try to put her gifts into words, but words cannot capture the level of excellence my tastebuds recollect.

Now back to you. Think about what your gift is and how you first discovered it. Think also about how you played with your gift and about how you and those nearby reveled in your excellence. When you see and feel the sensations associated with tapping into your gift, let your mind wander next to its status in terms of current opportunities where it can be applied, maybe even today. If you were an athlete and being an athlete brought you considerable enjoyment, health, and vibrancy, you can opt to revisit sports opportunities and find a parallel physical activity that matches your current time commitments, lifestyle, and demands. If your skill was public speaking, begin to search for opportunities where you can connect and inspire a group of people, such as in your workplace or in a volunteer organization.

Once you have a vision of how you wish to apply your gift in present life, write down what your skill is and your current vision of its potential application. Place the note on your refrigerator, with a second note placed on your work desk. The note should state, "I am . . ." The intention of the posting process is to remind you of your gift many times each day, while walking by and reaching for food or drink or when sitting down and working. After a few weeks of reflection, at most, sit down once more and develop a reasonable action plan and begin to put your gift into **action**. For a returning athletic pursuit, map out what equipment you need. Purchase equipment that excites you. If you are a runner, buy a new pair of flashy running shoes, comfortable running pants and shirt, and a running jacket. Next, set an activity calendar where you carve out time to reacquaint yourself with your gift, slowly but surely. A runner might then place running shoes at the door, just as a yoga enthusiast will either schedule virtual sessions into the day and have their yoga mat at the ready or engage a friend and go together to a yoga studio. A return to your gifts and how these are to be evoked needs to be, at first, a deliberate effort, until the gift is craved and automatically integrated into your daily life. Habits take time to form, so initially, every new behavior needs to be intentionally structured into your day. Then, be patient as you are challenged by the addition to your daily schedule. Remember, the application of your gifts must first smolder before they catch fire. Once a new application of your giftedness becomes routine, you will find it to be part of the evolving, next level, you. You might, at first, tap into your chosen gift—for example, cooking. You can plan out a few special meals each week and commit to experimenting and learning one new cooking technique each month. The uptake of your gift serves two purposes. Immediately, it brings you back in touch with a forgotten passion. Your passion will then serve to help you recognize other potential gifts that are just waiting to be tapped, meaning actions that come naturally to you and often have been known to you as early as childhood.

⏰ Lesson Reminders

- ❖ You have unique gifts that are innately yours—everyone does. You were born with these amazing gifts and can recall them from as far back as your childhood development. Remember to continuously recognize your gifts each day and to use them as often as possible. Using your gifts will reinforce that you are living as you should.

- ❖ When you tap into your gifts, you will feel in harmony. You will experience a personal recognition that you are doing what you are supposed to be doing in the way you are supposed to be doing it. As part of your insight, you will feel emotionally at peace with yourself and your surrounding world. So, tap into your gifts as often as you can. Through the consistent use of your own gifts, you will also serve as a model to other people nearby, who might model the concept of tapping into their gifts.

- ❖ At times, people and circumstances will challenge your use of the gifts that have always been your birthright. When you encounter situations where people tend to hide their gifts, stand firm and draw upon yours. You must always commit to bringing your gifts with you wherever you journey, no matter whether others in your environment choose to mute their gifts. Your gifts are meant to be enjoyed, so enjoy them.

❖ Share your gifts with others in your daily life. When you share your gifts, you also serve as a "gift leader" by setting a healthy example for the people around you. Tapping into personal giftedness provides an example that can spur equally healthy and monumental development in your family, friends, and colleagues. Encourage others to use their gifts, and in turn, they will support your giftedness.

LESSON TWO
FORCES

> *Two roads diverged in a wood and I—I took the one less travelled by, and that has made all the difference.*
>
> *Robert Frost*

A daily tension exists between confirming and challenging forces. One magnetic force is the intuitive and natural pull you feel when moving without resistance on your authentic path. A second competing force is experienced when you are challenged and you risk surrendering your optimal path to diverting demands and expectations, either from within you or by forces posed in your environment. These unnatural demands are recognized in the moments when you feel uncomfortable with a task, when you are acting out a role, or when you are involved in a discussion in a way that makes you think "this does not sound or feel like me."

Some of your days will be spent managing the competing and juxtaposed forces in your life. Competing forces, much like our gifts, begin early in life and stay with us throughout life's journey. In fact, your gifts and the competing forces away from your gifts are two parts of a whole. We are born with gifts. We gather a unique bank of experiences and value systems that are meant to assist with our reasoning and our decisions to tap into our potential. Some people are inclined toward artistry and various forms of creativity, but the external tendency in society is to choose conventional pathways that confine us to boxes we might not fit into. Some of us are natural debaters, and others respond best to agreement and reconciliation. These examples are internal forces that align with self-harmony, reminding us of who we are by our design.

As I shared in relation to my experiences in primary, secondary, and university schooling in lesson one, personal gifts and tendencies are sometimes questioned early in our lives. For example, many young children embarking on the vast selection of physical activities as versions of play have been guided into combative sports—ice hockey, track and field, or a diversity of other activities—often with an eager supporter signing them up. A parent might say, "My child should learn how to play golf or take up equestrian." The child, on the other hand, might have no interest in that activity. Perhaps you can remember a time when someone encouraged you to take up a hobby that didn't fit your interests or suit your personality. Far too often, people might not have a desire to enter the activity chosen for them, and they merely comply because family or friends are encouraging them to join and perhaps boxing them in. Since childhood I have been sensitive, quiet, and solitary. The sports I gravitated toward were individual unstructured activities such as grabbing a horse and jumping from field to field or running in the woods where I could set my own stride and pace. The external demand from the in-group among my peers during elementary school was full contact team sports played at recess, an option that did not at the time excite me. Because I was unsuited to these activities, I tended to be the last person chosen by my peers. Should I choose a preferred activity, a force pulling me back to my gifts, or should I opt for the in-group's preferred option, where I would experience tension from a lack of acceptance and lesser giftedness? How did you choose when faced with a similar set of options in youth or young adulthood? What are you choosing right now in relation to your preferred pathway—moving toward or away from it?

Understanding Forces

The pushes and pulls you have, and will continue to experience, in your life are not wrong. These frictions serve as reminders of the difference between a detour and a best-suited path. Even when people are engaged in their preferred activities, those they love, challenges can still arise where there are competing forces. Many elite performers wonder how to be accepted in their sports environment when their style of play and way of thinking and doing are regarded as unconventional by the coaches and athletes they train with daily. How can they be like their peers if their uniqueness and vision are juxtaposed from the norm? The most committed and self-assured people walk their path, disregarding the external forces pulling them toward what they consider personally unsuitable. Only the unique and most **resourceful** among us become stand-alones, meaning we push back against poorly matched demands and become world-class performers, the standouts we are meant to be. The best among us choose their own music, clothing, turn of phrase, leisure activities, career pursuits, and partners, not caring who may be listening and watching and not caring what others think of their decisions. The best of professional athletes and career professionals I've met and studied (12) have developed a strong sense of self and a thick skin. They understand that other people's judgments are ever-changing, without needing context and intimate knowledge of the reasoning behind their version of who they are as a performer. The best and most content among us follow our calling. Whether you use the term *vision, quest, North Star,* or any other common term, these euphemisms remind us to stay on the best-suited path rather than diverting to someone else's vision of who we should be and how it is we should live our lives.

The process of forging your own path and drawing on your internal forces is a daily pursuit. Each day brings its own promise, its own journey, and its own unavoidable tensions. From the moment you open your eyes to the time you close them at the end of each day, your hours will include activities, thoughts, and interactions involving a tension of forces, especially in the present computer age, where connectivity and rapid response are expected. Some days seem to last forever, with the minute hand practically unmoving despite your urging. Slow days, like frenetic days, are ones you know too well. Think of those days when you move from email message to message, phone call to phone call, and meeting to meeting, never reaching the bottom of the list or making progress in a task you want to complete. You might feel as if you are standing still instead of tapping into your creativity and skills. Drudgery and noncreative tasks can contribute to a sad state of human domestication in which people abide by prescribed rules and parameters such as a nine-to-five job in a profession they find boring and without value. However, each new day offers a new possibility to shift your perspective, revisit your priorities, and pursue the interests and applications you are excited to engage with. Think of each day in terms of heartbeats and breaths; think of the amount of time you savor life compared to the amount of time lost in disguise and wavering in your decisions. Time and life mileage are the most precious commodities of all human resources. The goal must be to spend as much time as possible invested in activities and behaviors and with people who confirm your gifts. Only these are immersive and treasured investments of your time and effort; only these choices can align with your potential for happiness and satisfaction on your correct path.

   Sports has always been a way to showcase how competing forces work. Every year, box office movies tell the stories of athletes who overcome life's hardships. The daily learning process and pathway of an Olympian or a professional athlete is built from tensions, progressions, setbacks, self-questioning, and recognitions (13). Peel back the lives of these athletes and even they regard their work at times as a daily grind, where passion might be displaced in the hours of blood, sweat, tears, and toil (14). Most elite athletes have expressed a feeling of forgetting about their love of the sport, as they place one foot in front of the other during daily training. The more successful athletes, however, are also process oriented (15), so they retrace quickly to the reasons for their pursuits, such as a childhood dream yet to be grasped. They think less of the drudgery required to strengthen their skills and more about their step-by-step progressions, savoring their learning and insight as much as each accumulated victory. Process-oriented performers are also able to delay gratification and to train patiently while reinforcing existing skills and techniques; only sometimes will they experience moments of expedited learning and development. The best athletes circle back often to who they wish to be and to their quest to move toward matching their gifts with their individuality as performer and person. It is far easier to remember who you are when your authentic personality and performance style match as you are sharpening existing gifts.

   The most gifted people are magnificently unique individuals, regardless of whether they eventually choose to reveal all or some of their individuality. If you share your uniqueness and remain open about who you are and what you stand for, you are equipped to weather the hardships in a career or life ambition of any sort. You can then move toward your version of excellence. Too many times people do not reveal their full selves to their friends, peers, colleagues, and broader society; instead, they become opaque—the opposite of transparent. The consequence of withholding their identities, which becomes a force drawing them away from their gifts, is dire in several ways. These people become average performers because they cannot bring all of themselves to their performances, where their person and performer become one and the same. Sometimes they conceal their identities and eventually are unable to perform their gifts due to a fear of revealing more than a partial, desired self throughout their development and performances. These people eventually wither away, as they lose self-worth and confidence. External forces can challenge and sometimes win over internal forces. When the battle is lost—perhaps because someone has suggested you are not as gifted as you thought, such as I experienced in high school at the hands of my sociology teacher—personhood and giftedness are at least temporarily vanquished.

Collaboration Is Key

Because of the challenges facing many world-class performers, I was compelled to undertake what became a well-profiled research study (15). Several Olympic athletes were asked how much of themselves they shared with their teams, meaning their peers and staff. Their responses varied, depending on individual fortitude and the degree of acceptance in each performer's sports discipline, meaning their training environment. Resolve was important, but so too was consistent support from coaches and supplemental staff (16). Those in supportive roles needed to understand that uniqueness is necessary in an athlete's pursuit of gifts because not all people hold the same gift. Neither do all people apply a familiar gift in a typical way because we are all individually unique. Two people might be equally talented writers, but they will bring different styles to their writing. How you choose to be and to interact with the people around you include the fullness of your identity, not just fragments—that is, only the imposed or anticipated desirable behaviors. Expectations or perceived norms can contribute to fractured bits and pieces of a much more formidable human being, outside and inside of performance. You must be fully you—nothing more, nothing less. When you are fully absorbed in the enjoyment of a task, that feeling you have is the feeling of being your complete self.

Performers committed to being themselves also associate with like-minded people in their performance environment, people who expect truthfulness from others and who are equally truthful on their respective paths as they tap into their own gifts. Athletes are often collaborative and need to be around people who understand and value truth and are interested in a shared version of how to exceed limits. No extraordinary performer can make it to the top in a solitary pursuit. Successful UFC fighters engage several people to work together in their preparation for each main event: a grappling coach, one who is an expert in striking; a mental performance coach; a physical coach; and perhaps a team leader who is a generalist with a broad-based knowledge of all the moving pieces. The people in the athlete's inner circle are expected to work as one army, upon whose shoulders the athlete can stand and launch to their delivery of excellence. Sadly, other athletes, like many employees, are gifted but place themselves in the hands of controlling mentors, such as a manager or adviser. These athletes soon feel and become lost; they no longer have daily access to sufficient creative and synergistic resources. They are challenged by lack of proper support to cover their needs. Either they find themselves in the middle of a tug of war, where they are pulled in many directions, or they feel smothered. The end result is a disassembled, isolated, and compromised performer instead of a person at peace who is able to live out and build upon existing gifts.

People seeking the transition to excellence should surround themselves with people who can work collaboratively each day so that the performer rises to become a more refined form than past or present. The best team is built with supporters who are egoless and able to join the athlete so that together they become a unified, mobilized beam of energy. When the team's vision becomes wide as opposed to narrow, the members of the team are willing and able to rein in one another's loss of focus or temporary distraction until the group returns to a commitment of reinforcing and magnifying the performer's uniqueness. Money does not buy cooperation or human performance, and authentic gifts are priceless, as many professional team owners or sport agents will agree when they feel they have overestimated, misjudged, or overspent. Many years ago it was discovered that a professional team's payroll does not predict their seasonal performance, especially after contracts have been solidified (17). An organization can pay for an employee's potential on paper, but cashing in on the investment of human giftedness is an entirely other discussion rarely considered and often left unharvested. Performance is something we, the performers, must want for ourselves and develop in ourselves, with support from those who are able and willing to help us develop a shared environment of excellence.

Normalizing Setbacks

During my formative years as a researcher, I found that world-class athletes, much like any other high-level performer, sometimes stall in their careers because of a single setback, a potential challenge, or a perceived unpassable barrier, which happened on a specific day in a specific performance (18). The result is a loss in pathway, but it also suggests a deeply flawed approach. Many athletes do not recover from their setbacks because they have chosen and been supported in delegating the responsibility for their loss to people or environments believed to be outside their control—that is, they externalize (19). Circumstances are not always under personal control—people hit speed bumps, they become ill, workplaces can dissolve, and relationships sometimes disintegrate. How we choose to face and process these moments requires a carefully designed and measured attempt at self-reflection, offering us the possibility of accountability, and only then, spurring further self-development (20). Accepting setbacks and events beyond your control is a necessary part of your growth in seeking a healthy resolution when you find yourself struggling. Sometimes you can achieve resolutions through self-reflection and recognition of your potential role in an incident or your response to it. In other scenarios you can benefit from a trusted family member, mentor, friend, colleague, or an ally ready to challenge your thinking and absolution. An efficient turnaround time and challenge to anger, fear, or sadness are often what people need most as opposed to acceptance of loss, the reinforcement of apathy, or the minimizing of a current situation by people meant to be supportive. You might find yourself in a challenging or uninspiring situation by circumstance, but you will remain there for indefinite periods of time by your own design (21).

Setbacks are often caused by systemic competing forces. One Olympic aspirant had a fractured support team, in which one team member chose not to work with the rest of the team staff in the athlete's final lead-up to a qualifying event. The athlete asked the group for emotional support in the quest to resolve a stumbling block—the lack of communication among staff. As those in the meeting listened to the saddened athlete traveling on a disintegrating pathway, several expressed a wish for this person's sadness, a symptom of a deeper problem, to dissipate.

While the upset athlete spoke, the others attempted to reassure the athlete but not to resolve the origin of the problem, which was the competing choice between forces of alienation or collaboration. I responded by encouraging the athlete to challenge the surrounding staff (those of us who were on the call) to work from a collaborative playbook, with the athlete prioritized over personal wants, needs, or past differences. The athlete could attempt to pull the staff together on a tight timeline, accept the fractured staff as inevitable, and work within the existing limitations, or she could reimagine the support network and take the necessary steps to engineer a modified team. The athlete was stuck at the epicenter of a stalled process and had to either choose the status quo or envision and then reengineer alternate resolutions. The status quo—the prevailing force pulling the athlete away from a synergistic team—took the athlete only so far toward her dream, where it could almost be touched but sadly remained out of reach. Often, the right path is in the short-term conflictual and uncomfortable, yet it is necessary to challenge an unhealthy structure in need of change. Plants sometimes need more nutrients in the soil, and sometimes they need to be repotted because the roots are unhealthy. Likewise, you might need to reconsider elements in your support team to ensure everyone is pulling in the same direction and the team is healthy.

Why We Debrief

Within a person's daily journey, just as in a longer-term career pursuit, the push and pull process of competing forces toward and away from your gifts can pose a challenge to what and how you perform. A day before I wrote this paragraph, my youngest son woke up in what he expressed as being "on the wrong side of the bed." He felt dislodged from his typical role of easygoing prankster. Though he slept well the night before, he was sad and disconsolate. The day was getting away from him. He was engaged in a day of e-learning due to a stay-at-home order and was unable to study, physically learn, and play with his friends. With each successive class, his eyes would well up time and again. When I tried to comfort him, he expressed he was having a sad day, as if the outcome was predetermined for that day, much like forecasted weather. Within the day's schedule was also time for play. He and I went outside and played basketball during one opportunity. During a second opportunity we played street hockey. Both instances revealed a very different side of my son—a joyful person. At the end of day, he and I sat at the foot of his bed and reflected on the day's events. We **debriefed**, as people always should, either during or after a day's journey. Our discussion was about his mood and every person's opportunity to switch from one mood and cluster of thoughts, contributive or debilitative, to another. Mood transitioning is like switching train tracks. We can shift our thoughts and emotions on the turn of a dime, even when we are not fully aware we are making a transition, much as a boxer who is down and out one moment can undertake a resurgence spurred by a single punch ending in victory. One minute we are carrying out one activity and struggling. The next minute we are fully invested in a second activity. What this shift in perspective reveals is that moods, which are linked to our thoughts, can be fleeting depending on our response to competing forces. When we are mired in frustration, anger, or sadness, there is less room for an alternative, healthier response. At times it is appropriate to feel disappointment and to think through a present personal struggle. Where did it originate, and why? However, as we self-question, we should also consider how much time is necessary to make sense of the competing forces we are grappling with and when is it the right time to act decisively and make productive changes to our conditions.

Choices are easy enough to make, verbalize, and execute when we dig down into who we are and how we wish to be and ignore the varying propensities of those who surround us. Our Olympian efforts can only be achieved when we choose a path in alignment with our natural gifts and abilities and a supporting cast who also align with us. Many people could become Olympic champions or professional sports greats, but sadly they never climb their own podiums. Similarly, there are people in every workplace who could give and become much more than they are. Some people are born leaders but stay hidden in the shadows, choosing not to apply for leadership opportunities. Others could be more supportive of their colleagues. Each has chosen not to fight hard enough, long enough, or with consistency for the forces that would have served to magnify their natural gifts. People sometimes take what appears in the short-term to be the easy way out, the path of least resistance, and give in to forces, such as one's unique and innovative workstyle, that little by little pull them away from the effective use of a gift. Paths to success are forged in steely decisions each day. Whether we choose to draw on our gifts and learn from the competing forces surrounding us is a question of free will. You might choose to reinforce and fortify your path, or you might choose an alternate counterintuitive pathway and bend yourself to unhealthy influences.

By being aware and by checking in throughout the day, you can follow the opportunity to reinforce your desired path or alter a path that is perhaps misaligned with your gifts. People living and using their unique gifts need to also understand who they are and who they are not and then choose to invest in the territory of their gifts. Advocating for your gifts is a daily opportunity that will reaffirm who you are each time you advocate and strengthen your commitment to be exactly where you should be in your progression. To summarize, you have gifts. These gifts are ones you have known about for quite some time. When your gifts are nourished, they will serve as opportunities to strengthen your natural skills and your resolve. Hopefully, you are also becoming more aware of the potential competing forces in your life that pull you away from your gifts. You know exactly what it feels like and how you react when you move away from your natural gifts and live a part of your life in an unnatural way. The insights from lesson two now lead into the next action, where you will be asked to map out your competing forces.

Action Item Two: Identifying Your Gifts and Forces

You were asked to consider your gifts as I spoke about mine in lesson one. Although you have several wonderful gifts, there are always competing forces pulling you toward and away from them. Now it's time to examine your gifts and the pushes and pulls relating to a few of your gifts. For step one, open your computer or pull out a pad of paper. Return to what we discussed in lesson one and write down your gifts in block letters. Writing each gift in block letters is meant to remind you that you are the holder of your wonderful gifts. When listing the gifts, start with an easy one—the one in the forefront of your mind. If I were to think of a gift at this very second, while writing this task, authoring comes to mind. There are certain gifts in the forefront of your mind too. Think a little more about your life and some of the other wonderful gifts that are starting to come to your mind. You might be gifted in your profession. If you are in architect, perhaps your creativity as an architect is a logical one to list. You can list a few work-related gifts. The lawyer might list being a gifted litigator and a talented negotiator. Both these gifts are vastly different—one advocating for a position and the other bringing diverse opinions together into a mutually acceptable win–win scenario.

Now that you have your work gifts listed, look beyond this one part of your existence to other gifts, such as athleticism. You may be a fantastic golfer, squash player, or tennis player. One or a few of these activities might be currently used to let off steam and to keep you fit. Despite why you are engaging in them, you have some raw or developed talent in the recreational activity. Now what relational gifts do you have? One of your strengths might be the ability to relate with people to the point where they feel comfortable around you. You have this wonderful gift of making people really feel happy in your presence. You might also be highly creative and artistic—able to see and create art or see a problem or a topic from a unique vantage that benefits not only you but the people you meet. You get the picture. Now let your pen flow and develop your list.

Step two is to take a color highlighter if writing on paper and circle the gifts you are looking to press into action now or soon, such as within the next six months. If you are working from a laptop or tablet, change the font of gift from black to a vibrant color and bold the words. As you choose the gifts to prioritize, make certain that those you select cover more than one part of your life. The person overly focused on work might tend to choose more gifts from the work part of life. Choose gifts that draw on at least three different parts of your life—your personal, recreational, and work segments. Choosing at least one important gift from each area will encourage you to think in symmetry, a topic we will cover later in lesson seven. Now that you have listed your gifts that cover different but important parts of your thriving life, look at these and make certain you have all the prioritized gifts you wish to work toward.

Now comes the fun part. In step three, you get to identify the competing forces that take you toward strengthening each gift as well as the counterforces that challenge its growth to full potential. Tackle this challenge one gift at a time and do not rush through step three. Expect that step three might require you to step away from the exercise today and return to it tomorrow. Instead of rushing through your evaluation of forces for each gift, do them one at a time and be totally honest with yourself in terms of what the competing forces are. Perhaps one of your gifts is that you are a great tennis player. You were an elite tennis player in your youth, and now you play tennis for fun with friends. Though you love to play tennis and it brings you so much joy, you rarely get to play anymore. Time just doesn't permit it. You have a work schedule, a consulting business, family demands, and you feel exhausted at the end of each day because you have lost some of your fitness over time by sitting in front of a desk. All these examples are forces that pull you away from more regular tennis matches and all that they could bring to your life. There are also forces that attract you to tennis, ones that pull you back to play, albeit for fewer matches than you wish. Just the same, these forces are forces of attraction. A force of attraction might be that you feel wonderful when you are on the court. You also really enjoy battling against your friends and colleagues; tennis ignites your inner competitor. Another attraction is when you finally pull the trigger and schedule in and play tennis, you are able to move and focus on your passion without thinking of any of life's stresses. Now take the time and work through each of your gifts and come up with your own dueling forces.

Step four is your opportunity to do a deep dive and examine any reasoning that explains each force. Let's return to the person who loves to play and is an extremely gifted tennis player but is struggling with regularly scheduling in the activity. The person exploring the reasoning for the scheduling struggle (one of the counterforces) might conclude that it is not prioritized because it doesn't pay the bills. It's a discretionary activity. If one activity must be dropped from the weekly schedule, it might as well be a discretionary activity as opposed to cutting back on work demands. Another reason against playing tennis might be that workdays are full and there is little left to give by the end of the day, other than to family. If we dig a little deeper than that, we might find feelings of guilt and shame associated with taking care of oneself and prioritizing health and fitness when there are lots of commitments waiting to be done around the house. Just as the counterforces exist, the deeply rooted reasoning supporting the forces of attraction also exists. For example, the tennis player needs to move their body and regain some of the fitness lost because of work demands and unbalanced time scheduling, which eventually leads to compromised physical health. The person realizes that the body is craving movement and a good, regular sweat. Dig a little deeper and you might hear that when the person schedules in and carries through with the activity, the rest of that day is harmonious. The person brings the best to a partner, children, friends, and coworkers and also sleeps well and feels great! Write down and look at your deeply rooted arguments to understand the pushes and pulls toward and away from each gift.

The fifth and final step brings you back to each gift and all the surrounding work you have done to understand what is pulling you toward and away from a balance of your gifts. Remember, you are examining the ones you prioritized from at least three parts of your life, not just one. Now that you have done the heavy work associated with each gift, what have you learned about how you are approaching each prioritized gift? By examining the words you have written in relation to each, you will gain a good sense of why it is or isn't flourishing. For the gifts that are flourishing, take note that you have built some pretty good forces of attraction that have overruled the counterforces. With those that are working well, all that needs to be done is for you to recognize how you have worked in favor of the gift. You have made good decisions to build and polish the gift. Recognizing why these gifts are flourishing can teach you a lot about what you need to do in relation to gifts that are less developed or overlooked. For the gifts that are meaningful to you but aren't flourishing, what barriers have you developed to block regular access to the gift? Your creation of barriers might have been intentional or unintentional, but they are barriers just the same. Look at these barriers and recognize them for what they are—potential bad decisions. This exercise may result in confirmation or frustration, depending on the gift being examined. No matter your response, you are now aware of the forces at play in your life, why they are working as they are, and how they relate to your trade-offs. Understanding your gift-based decisions will set the stage for the next lesson, which explores what happens when gifts are set aside.

⏰ Lesson Reminders

- ❖ Forces are internal and external demands and expectations that seek to pull us toward our gifts or take us away from them. These forces are a natural part of your daily existence and human condition. Confirming forces are ones that will draw you toward the use of your natural gifts, whereas challenging forces will take you away from tapping into your potential.

- ❖ You will experience dueling forces in your daily life. It is impossible to avoid the competing forces that draw you toward and away from your gifts. You will know when you are off course because you will feel either frustrated, unmotivated, or both. You may also feel incomplete in terms of the qualities you are bringing to your daily life. Forces counter to your gifts limit your potential.

- ❖ Each day, be deliberate in your choices between competing forces, whether created by you or someone else. The competing force might be a task that runs counter to who you are, or it might be a way of interacting with people. As you learn to recognize when competing forces are at play in your life, choose to play to your strengths and your gifts. If you are a logical and systematic thinker, take the time to formulate logical responses as opposed to making rash decisions.

- ❖ A certain hardening process is necessary when choosing between competing forces that bring you closer or take you farther from your gifts. Become well skilled as your own personal advocate when it comes to making life decisions. Although awareness is a great starting point, daily actions are necessary to strengthen your ability to opt for well-aligned forces and opt out of those that don't match with the delivery of your gifts. Remember that challenges make you stronger.

LESSON THREE
CONTORTIONS

> *There is no greater agony than bearing an untold story inside you.*
>
> Maya Angelou—I Know Why the Caged Bird Sings

You journey through life with a personal compass to evaluate competing forces—that is, forces that indicate when you move toward or away from your gifts. Your thoughts and behaviors can be influenced by the world around you, and they can alter or mute your gifts to the point at which you become contorted. Contortions happen to everyone. They occur when you apply an untruthful version of yourself in one or more parts of your daily life. For example, one of your gifts might be that you are a wonderfully empathetic person, kind to others, and tuned into their needs and their feelings. Yet, for a time, maybe influenced by internal circumstances or the people nearby, this wonderful part of you can become muted or left unpracticed. By letting go of your gift, you act in a way that does not match your values, personality, and the tendencies you like most within yourself.

Contortion and Youth

In my neighborhood I have noticed a common sort of contorting. Certain children are beginning to struggle with how they dress, speak, and act—a crisis of self-questioning that for them has begun at a young age. Some of the young are on a quest to fit in. The external demands on impressionable children and youth, originating from schoolmates, family, and social media, are overwhelming and consistently present. These young people hover over their smartphones or other devices in churches, at bus stops, and even while studying in class. They even communicate with the person in the next seat by sending a text message instead of making eye contact and speaking. Chances are this description sounds all too familiar. These children are a formidable example of how some people in many societies, particularly in developed nations, contort from who they know themselves to be when they are most at home inside their own skin.

Young people on every street, from an early point in their lives, respond to competing social expectations of who they are and should be by placing value in their physical self and how they come across to their peers as highly desirable commodities. Clothes are a revealing expression of how they package themselves to be socially acceptable in this competitive world. Considerable time may be spent on hair, facial regimes, makeup, brand-name clothing, the right shoes, sunglasses, electronic devices, transportation, and other possessions. If our youth really wish to conform, they may adopt a vogue but developmentally unsuitable conversation and language. Packaged-up youth searching for a quick transition to adulthood find themselves in vulnerable life moments, moments that pass—especially in modern society—almost with the blink of an eye. They initially believe they are on a happy and positive course keeping up with what is currently trending. Some people will nod approval and support, suggesting the rapidly changing youth are on the correct path and moving at the correct pace. The youth are then reinforced in the idea they are looking and playing their part as acceptable members in a commercialized world. These youth can also dramatically alter their personas in ways they believe further add to their desirability. Since the beginning of time some follow such a path and grow up faster than they are ready for. Societal pressures and expectations wage a perilous battle against the authenticity for these young persons' souls during an important life stage, when personalities are being formed and life paths are being considered.

Self-assured children may not be the most popular in their youth, but they quickly become aware (some painfully, some peacefully) that they are a counterculture to their commercialized peers. Children and youth who walk to their own beat and dance to their own drum hopefully remain content with their decision—that is, in knowing they stand apart from many of their friends. With the support of like-minded peers from school, social clubs, and engaged family members, they are forging their true path while learning how to buffer against the external pressures to be someone or something they intuitively know they are not by nature. These self-assured children are not unlike adults, who are equally aware of the societal pressure to look and speak a certain way, to improve their physique, to drive the right car, to live in the right neighborhood, and to travel to the right vacation destinations. Although these challenges, beginning with children, are immense in the short term, the rewards of their hard-fought choices to stand their ground and remain resolved will be long-standing. Like trees, children must develop deep roots to weather the storms ahead and to draw their nourishment from healthy soil as they grow. When trees grow too quickly and without proper deep rooting, they eventually dry up from dehydration and become malnourished. Eventually they wither and starve, or they fall over with the first gust of a heavy wind or pounding rain. The answers to growth sometimes are found in deeper soil; likewise, people should sometimes grow their roots a little deeper than they do. Young people know, based on feeling and intuition, what their right path should be, if only they would devote time to consider their course. Similarly, internal warning signals like uncertainty and confusion warn our youth when they begin to deviate from who, what, and where they should be.

Contortion and the Workplace

The workplace is a second environment where people run the risk of contorting into false or muted versions of themselves based on external pressures to conform. Consider this scenario: In a job interview, you are asked about your personal hopes and dreams. The question is a typical one we have all been asked when being interviewed for a job, a promotion, or a transfer. I was asked this question during my initial interview at the university I have worked for my entire career. Having been denied a few academic positions during my job search, and with a pending sense I would be moving from one sport contract to the next for years to come, my wife and I sought stability as a cornerstone in our life together. I walked into the interview room and knew I had nothing to lose and everything to gain by showing my hand and being myself. I answered based on how I truly believed I could contribute to the group and organization, one I had studied carefully beforehand. I expressed my desire to be internationally recognized as a scholar and to help others on faculty with their own advancement. We could be partners in the workplace, sharing in the bounty of international recognition. I also wanted to continue as a motivational consultant to Olympic and professional athletes. I shared a vision in which, as a faculty member,

I could contribute as a social scientist and as a societal leader to my field at an international level and to bring worldwide connections to my university, my colleagues, and our prospective students. The response to my impassioned plea from the committee around the table, finally, was outright enthusiasm. I had met my perfect match—we were simpatico. Those on the hiring committee were excited by the person in front of them, and I saw the recognition of a bright shared future in their eyes. Their hope was that we would be stronger together than each of us without the other. I was to become a valuable contributor and an agent of positive change in my workplace. The people before me were mostly strong educators and administrators. To them I was a versatile, receptive, and highly approachable educator, scientist, and practitioner. I also liked the sorts of hobbies and outdoor life known and relished by my future colleagues.

Although I was attractive to the hiring committee based on my energy and vision, I also represented something foreign and perhaps a little frightening. People who bring new ideas and a larger or unfamiliar scope of vision to those nearby often will be seen as a potential cause for uncertainty and change to the status quo. I represented a potential next-generation employee who not only was engaged and broad visioned but also was different from many in this unfamiliar work environment. These generous colleagues emphasized their teaching almost entirely with undergraduate students. They spent countless hours in individual meetings with each student throughout the students' undergraduate experiences. Although I also devoted much of my earlier years in the organization to meetings and student–faculty social events, the approach was not sustainable, assuming I wished to remain steadfast to my own developmental path as a social scientist and as a person committed to supporting elite athletes. I understood the organization I was joining, with all its charms and limitations, weighed against some of my natural strengths and interests, yet I chose to proceed. The fit was right, and the people were kind and caring. I also steeled myself for the competing forces ahead—those that would play to my strengths counterbalanced with those that might delay my own vision of international professional. My concerns included staff resistance to the time I invested in research, publishing, and graduate students—the ingredients needed to build one's reputation to a national level. I also feared an overemphasis on small administrative tasks such as unnecessary meetings, social in nature, that might consume valuable time, when instead I could help support a stronger science-to-practice culture in the department. The process of steeling ourselves is something we all must do when seeking to contribute positive change and a new perspective to an existing organization, whether in a workplace, a volunteer organization, a sport team, or in any environment where people regularly collaborate.

Most of us begin our employment positions with dreams of how we can contribute in the most amazing ways to a better workplace, a better profession, or a more productive society. As new workplace hires, we quickly learn a considerable amount about our place of employment. Firsthand experiences are gained through job demands, which become known when your feet hit the ground running and you work hard to learn the tasks and understand the organization. Within my university, I taught with enthusiasm and had an open-door policy to students, parents, faculty, leadership, and the media to promote the link between my teaching, my research, and my experience with elite sports. No task was too small or too large for me to accept and master. On the one hand, I was grateful for the employment opportunity and to the university for having believed in me enough to see potential that others had missed. I did my best for my colleagues and my organization, developing personal skills while fostering growth in colleagues and the student body. On the other hand, I did not want to confine myself to teaching and committee work, because doing so would have misshaped me and resulted in yet another dissatisfied employee in yet another workplace. There was, however, considerable pressure to align who I was with the status of the organization.

All organizations live, breathe, and evolve. Despite pressure to conform, I charted my own course and tapped into my natural gifts as opposed to modifying my vision of who I wanted to become. Had I relented, I would have never mentored doctoral students; undertaken scientific research relating to local indigenous sports participation or researched cultural inclusion in elite sport psychology; pursued international societal leadership, a federally endowed research chair, senior editorial board positions, or distinguished international professorships; or traveled to Olympic and professional sports events (22). I would have become a clone of other equally valuable but comparatively different professionals. I would have become a familiar and entirely malleable entity, unrecognizable to myself and those I loved. The consequence has been that I am entirely satisfied with my career path! There were always competing forces in my work life; in fact, there always will be. However, I choose to be true to myself and play to my strengths regardless of competing options. When my workday ends, I bring my satisfied self to my partner and my children, who must be supported on their respective pathways.

To some degree, your work experience parallels mine, at least in terms of the pressures and expectations. You have thoughts about how your competing forces align with who you perceive yourself to be as a professional, regardless of the occupation and worksite you have chosen. We all begin our new positions with hopes and dreams, wishing to be a valued member of a team and organization while remaining true to who and what we are. The challenge in relation to your desired pathway is what has or will happen to you and your ambitions as a contributing employee over time. Consider the following questions: Have you remained equally engaged and visionary in your workplace environment from day one until today? Have you delivered or overdelivered on your initial commitments? The clock has been ticking, with days turning into months, years, or decades. Do you continue to recognize the best version of yourself in your workplace as you support the people you work with and your organization?

No workplace is perfect. It's unrealistic to expect perfection in your changing organization or the people who work within its walls. However, you must continue to envision and demand the best from yourself and those around you and continue to serve as a healthy force in your jobsite. Far too many people hope the shine and the luster of their workplace will endure without being consistently engaged. They expect positive changes and positive movement to happen without any effort on their part. Yet, the meaning of work, without sustained engagement and a consistent contribution to success, will evaporate until it is ordinary and you become equally ordinary despite being uniquely gifted. Just as you look to your environments to nourish you, you hold equal responsibility to nourish people in your workplace and to share your unique skill sets and gifts to help enrich those around you each day. You are one person, but a single gifted person holds tremendous power to change an entire environment. You hold the opportunity to harvest your gifts and apply them to your organizational environment, thereby becoming an emblem for transformative change. I believe my influence was transformative to faculty who now publish and supervise doctoral students, where otherwise they might not have done so. Their lives grew in tandem with my own.

Contortion and Sports

It would be easy to fall into the trap of thinking one person does not change the inspiration and productivity of a group. Yet, many examples suggest the contrary. Each story in this section reinforces the concept that you can influence the people around you by modeling excellence. For example, consider any story in which a professional athlete is traded to a new team. The team might have underachieved and suffered a performance drought before the new arrival suddenly ignited the group, culminating in the group's elevated success. Within male ice hockey, Wayne Gretzky was traded from the Edmonton Oilers to the Los Angeles Kings (23), and Mark Messier was traded to the New York Rangers (24). Both players led their respective teams to the Stanley Cup Finals in their first year of assignment to their new organization. One person can change the wider landscape of a sport or field. For example, without the trade of Wayne Gretzky from a Western Canadian City to the Sunbelt in the United States (23)—in this instance, California—ice hockey would have likely continued with little fandom and no brand recognition in a large demographic region. Not only did Gretzky contribute to his team's success but also to the success of ice hockey as a whole. Since the trade, California alone supports three National Hockey League teams, each **thriving**. Although these individuals could have easily seen their new assignment as their daily job and not made a connection with their teammates and local communities, the ripple effect of their passion and how influential it was could never have touched the many people now engaged in their love of ice hockey. An individual grain of sand is all that is needed to tip the balance of any scale. You can be that grain of sand in any achievement setting or life opportunity you choose. See the potential meaning behind your decision and recognize the power you have when your personal gifts are being pressed into action, not only for your benefit but also for the benefit of many. Take your gifts and share them, serving as a positive force in your environment.

Despite the positive influence sports athletes can have on those in their surrounding area, they, like you, are not immune to the pressure of contorting and misplacing their gifts. A boxer I was working with faced misaligned advice in advance of a global media press conference. External influences wanted the boxer to be more assertive and get in his opponent's face—to be aggressive and intimidating—as a tactic for success. The belief was that the opponent needed to fear and respect this boxer based on behaviors displayed at the press conference, which would translate into the opponent being intimidated within the ring. The opponent was by his very nature, a bully; he was also the reigning world champion. The boxer initially acted like a bully equivalent to the reigning champion. However, my client is a kind soul, and his gifts of introspection and patience always served him well throughout an accomplished, ascending, and illustrious boxing career. He is a thinking athlete, one who is measured and strategic in his craft. Trying to be abrasive and openly aggressive was neither intuitive nor a natural engagement of his talents or gifts compared to the opponent he faced. Moreover, he was a boxer and not a brawler, so, he and his team revisited our strategic approach in alignment with the athlete's true gifts. We supported the athlete so that he, in turn, could play to his own strengths, those that came naturally to him, those he would be able to pull out of the hat under pressure.

There is a distinction in the sport of boxing between boxers and brawlers. Sugar Ray Leonard was a boxer able to overcome most brawlers. Mike Tyson was known to be a brawler who was able to out-brawl most boxers. When a boxer tries to be a brawler, or a brawler tries to be a boxer, they will find themselves in metaphorical deep water, unable to tap into their personality, style, rhythm, and conviction during a performance. Knowing his true temperament and obvious athletic and intellectual gifts, I encouraged the boxer to remain his measured and humble self during the press conference. He was not baited into engaging with his opponent with a false representation of himself, thereby trying to fight fire with fire. Instead, his opponent, lacking appropriate insight, made the faulty assumption that my client's measured behavior equated with intimidation and the patience he displayed during the press conference signified submission. The action in the ring told an entirely different story than the champion and crowd saw coming. Over 12 rounds the boxer artfully reduced his brawling opponent to bewilderment and then sad recognition. A well-placed jab was followed by a strategic punch combination, which was then followed by a slick movement, during which he never deviated from his plan, his style of person, or his innate speed, agility, and intelligence. Recognizing and aligning gifts and not succumbing to external forces based on suggestions of who one should be will always foster excellence. When the person and the performance unify, the result is truthful, easiest to deliver, and rewarding in the experience, given that it is confirming. The athlete, the coaches, the staff, and the fans can all discern true from untrue and what is clear from what is distorted and misaligned.

Movement away from one's natural gifts and contortion are common. Many athletes model themselves after experienced and successful opponents to copy their icons and, by extension, their pathway to success. When athletes deviate from their personal tendencies built around personalized gifts, they alter who they are and what works best for them and forgo a tried, well-suited pathway to success that is built around the uniqueness of their gifts. I have watched athletes in warm-up areas at Olympics, world championships, and in highly televised public exhibitions watch a better-known athlete warm-up and then try to emulate the same process, even using the same facial expressions and posture. The athletes who try unwisely to become someone else—they act as impostors rather than themselves—are hard-pressed to find their groove during their warm-up. These same athletes underachieve because it is virtually impossible to effectively emulate someone else under pressure; duplication of another person is never deeply rooted within us. Emulating another person is a fine compliment to the person being modeled, but most often it takes the performer far afield from the gifts they have and how these should be pressed into action. Many paths lead to excellence, and they are as unique as the exceptional performers at the apex of their sports, the entrepreneurs at the summit of exceptional businesses, and the scientists at the precipice of cutting-edge discoveries. You can learn a lot in terms of persistence and even tactical strategies by watching the best of the best in your employment field, in your hobby, or in your personal life, but they are not you and you are not them. Instead of glancing sideways and watching other top-class performers, something many susceptible athletes do, you must look inward, value your uniqueness, and deliver your version of performance. Each performance you deliver is a new performance of you, building on your existing physique, personality, and style of play. There are many versions of excellence, and your version needs to be the one you invest in and then follow. Flow with the river's current; that is, allow your version of excellence to flow out of you so that you can express your true self.

Prioritizing Authenticity

When you lose direction and contort in any part of your life, you will intuitively know by gut instinct and your emotional reaction that you are on a wrong path. However, you might lack strategies or know how to redirect your efforts, perhaps compounded by a lack of guidance (or unsuitable guidance) from people you trust, such as a training partner or colleague. Feelings of frustration and confusion can fuel the uncertainty you are facing. These insufficiencies make it challenging to fight your way back to your true version of performance. Next, you may begin to suffer from a loss of self-growth caused by destructive understanding about your performance and from feelings of hopelessness (25) that will stagnate your insight, your progression, and the best application of your gifts. Anyone can focus on the obstacle before them with sufficient time and willingness to resolve their current compromised self. We have all stalled out in one way or another, likely more times than we can remember. So, when you have performed contorted, you must uncover where you missed the mark in terms of execution. When you understand the loss, you can move beyond the setbacks and resume life as it is meant to be for you with a deeper knowledge and appreciation of who you are, of those in your performance environment, and of the environment in general.

When you experience a setback caused by contortion, a proper debriefing process that you can follow and track is beneficial (26). When did you stop being you, and when did you began taking on some other role? Widen the discussion to the people you trust—maybe two to three key people. Assign a note taker so all ideas are captured on paper or an electronic device. Each trusted member will have a personal vantage point, knowing you as you and having witnessed your performance setback. By sharing multiple perspectives, you will gain a broader understand of the setback, the flawed decisions you and those involved made in relation to your gifts, and the daily logistic planning decisions that were not useful based on who you are and how you perform. Think of that interview or important meeting where you were not quite yourself. Perhaps you are typically confident, well spoken, a good listener, and a collaborator, but you were suddenly assertive and perhaps dismissive of another person's ideas. The person you were in that moment is unusual, but did your behavior happen out of thin air? Were there small things that happened and small decisions you made that led to this different version of you? Using these steps, you can begin to debrief by examining your central role in your loss of the tendencies you are most gifted with. Did you cut back on sleep? Did you nourish and drink enough fluids before the meeting? Did you take enough time to clear your mind before the important meeting and so on? Next, involve people who know you well and are truthful to help you further explore the chain of events. This will help you find where you contorted, how you contorted, and why you contorted. This is a simple lesson, but it will also be a long-standing reminder (providing you learn from your contortion) for subsequent opportunities of how to be the best version of yourself in a group meeting.

Contortions happen, but the question is whether the results of the contortion will have a long-term effect on your way to deeper gifts? Many years ago, I embarked on a research project, a necessary component needed to complete doctoral studies and a step needed to close the chapter of my equestrian career while continuing my path. I was a recently retired international athlete who never achieved my potential of becoming an Olympian, though I was at certain points relatively close. Reflecting upon my experiences (not with sadness but with wisdom and gratitude), I recognized I sometimes self-sabotaged. I tended to be susceptible to the suggestions and guidance of anyone within earshot, despite having a very good coach and strong analytical skills beyond my years. I wanted to seek acceptance, and I confused the reception of opinions with signs of friendship. When I listened to the wide number of incoming suggestions, I became confused about how my version of athlete and person were one. My thoughts and ideas were diluted, and I was unrecognizable from the person I knew myself to be at the core. There were other moments of shining brilliance in my athletic career when I bested world champions. There were days and a few memorable seasons when I listened to myself and found ways through challenges based on who I was. I worked quietly about my business and paid little attention to the progression of my competitors. I competed against myself, and in so doing, focused exclusively on my own evolution. My performance reflected this internal harmony of self with my equine partner. However, these moments or periods of time were typically followed by performances far from my best, where I was unable to complete a sporting event, or if I did, only to an average standard and the middle of the pack. The tension between personal judgment and self-questioning culminated in a compromised style of performance, one which rendered me mechanical, stiff, and without instinct, intuition, and artistry.

Eventually, my time was running out and I needed a change in landscape to rediscover existing gifts and to gain a fresh start. At retirement, knowing about this precarious game of lost and found in the search for performance excellence, I transposed my earlier experience of being a gifted but inconsistent performer into a doctoral research topic. I tried to understand why some national team athletes lose and recover their international level skills with ease, others falter only for a time due to abandonment and eventual rediscovery of their gifts, and some never regain their original swagger due to a lack of effective internal resources, such as knowing how to take responsibility for a mistake or how to reflect on one's mistakes systematically with support from the people around them (27). The three examples of discovery or lack of discovery crystalized how any performer's path can be lost and only sometimes found during battles waged between internal knowledge, external human resources, and their reconciliation into a personally successful formula. Sometimes the two understandings come together, contributing to a better-developed version of what already comes naturally—nourishing one's gifts. Other times, people who achieve greatness as part of a treasured life must rely on intuition and personal judgment to help navigate through their confusion, eventually reaffirming and strengthening the person they know themselves to be.

What can be learned from this study so many years later? The minute you transition in how you work and play, you become untrue to your unique and authentic origin, one familiar to you. The person and the action should be inseparable, but sometimes they diverge as people begin to modify themselves against their better judgment. Be who you are in all aspects of your life, be it work, sport, or play. The person (you) who became a success story can only continue to grow in success by staying on their (your) path. I have suggested until now that the loss of an authentic pathway happens over time. Contortions happen easily enough. If they happen in one area of your life, it is possible that giving way to influences will permeate to further parts of your life and spill over to influence the life quality and even the life habits of those you love most dearly. The gradual turning away from a valued path is sometimes hard to spot until you are so far into a flawed journey your patterns, including ways of thinking, surrounding arguments, and behaviors, reinforce and imprison you in misadventure, where you find yourself in foreign territory. Just as it takes time to travel down a path not yours, it also takes courage, willingness, time, and patience to retrace your steps; learn the necessary lessons; reconsider your understanding of events; and revise your direction with improved understanding of who you are and what personally works best. Journeys away from your true self are often dismissed as wasted time. However, what you make of your life experiences defines you, ideally for the better, and makes you stronger. If you come out of a contorted experience or process with better understanding and insight regarding who you are, who you should be, and where you should move to, your future will be bright. The important takeaway from this lesson is to remember who you are each day by checking in with your gifts, your gut instincts, and whether the two complement each other. Understand and appreciate that your life course will sometimes include losing your true path. Each diversion is its own opportunity to rediscover and further strengthen you, moving you ever closer to who you are meant to be. Although listening to external suggestions is important, as a renowned client told me in a quiet moment before a major sporting event, the performer's role can include an invitation for feedback, but the ultimate decision in terms of your path should be made by the person at the epicenter of the decision—you—and not an advisory panel.

⚠ Action Item Three: Identifying and Understanding Your Contortions

Having completed the active engagement exercise for the first lesson you should have reacquainted yourself with your gifts and begun to consider an action plan on how to reengage with what makes you gifted. The action exercise in the second lesson required you to complete a mapping exercise, highlighting the internal and external forces present in your life, and encouraged you to develop counters to these forces. This present exercise is designed to help you identify your contortions. As you may have moved away from your original gifts over the years or have experienced the push and pull of forces, you have also learned to contort by subscribing to false expressions of your true self. One of the most important elements to rediscovering your path is to identify and understand your current contortions. Who or what has influenced you away from your gifts, and who or what can help bring you back to your center?

For this exercise you will need a notepad and pencil. Find a quiet time in your day, with no interruptions from ringing cell phones, demands from loved ones and colleagues, or visual cues of work to be done. For example, I wouldn't attempt this exercise while at the kitchen table with unopened mail in sight or near children or loved ones seeking my attention. Once you have found the location and set aside the time to fully commit to this exercise, identify the most important aspects of your life, writing down each one on its own line. Some readers may identify people, such as your closest friends and family members, your employer, your coach, or trainer. Other readers may list a spouse or partner; an organization you love volunteering with; a spiritual group you attend; a society you belong to; or an activity you engage in on a regular basis, such as yoga, running, cycling, rowing, music, or theater. When you are finished listing your treasured items, you will likely have 5, 10, 20, or more line items of meaningful and influential activities, people, or organizations that bring out your giftedness.

Take a moment to think about the gifts you identified in part one of this exercise. Close your eyes and envision yourself embracing each of these activities as gifts relating to where you want to go as a person. Look at your list; line by line, evaluate each activity, person, and organization with sharp attention to how they can contribute to and support you on your true path toward your fullest life. Is the friend you identified on line five a person who would support the progressive changes you currently want to make, or would you feel embarrassed or shy to discuss your plans with this friend? Is the family member identified on line 12 someone you can rely on to push you further and catch you when you stumble in your quest for excellence, or are they more inclined to judge your missteps and discourage your attempts to excel? Consider the organization you identified on line 17. Does this establishment further your forward momentum and provide opportunities for you to tap into your gifts, or does your involvement with them take you farther from your path, causing you to contort into someone you really don't care for all that much—one who is not performing as you should at the top of your game?

This is a thought-provoking evaluative exercise. You are examining the very fabric of your current life—stitch by stitch, activity by activity—through a new lens focused on affirming and rediscovering the places and company around which you can embrace your gifts. Some of the people, places, or things you previously engaged with may no longer be part of the fabric of who you are after you reflect on what you are doing and with whom. That is okay. This is an exercise of taking stock and making the necessary changes to ensure you have the optimal environments in which to thrive day by day in support of your journey.

Let me provide you with an example from an elite setting. I have worked with many professional athletes, and the best of these have sought opportunities that came with considerable pressure, huge audiences, and a lot of accountability. The best of these athletes are highly resourceful people. Their teams include coaches, sport science staff, medical staff, a sports agency, public relations specialists, and so on. My relationships with many of these athletes have spanned decades, and so I have watched them add and take away members of their team based on whether the staff member adds value to the team and their quest to exhibit their giftedness on the sports stage. I have seen coaches replaced by new coaches, agents substituted, and strength and conditioning coaches replaced. The best performer is very much in tune with mind and body. They know who is helping to fuel their dreams and who has transitioned into being a naysayer. These athletes are looking for synergy within their team. The changes they make contribute to dynamic teams that contribute positive synergy and improved technical and tactical information. The athletes are looking for the resources they need given the challenges before them, taking into consideration their current developmental strengths and the parts of their gifts requiring a little more polish. It is a sort of mix-and-match process.

This analogy also applies to you. As you will discover throughout this book, when you gain the best possible support toward bringing out and delivering your gifts, your supporters are resources with specialized skills and not static people to rely on. This exercise asks you to examine your resources and evaluate them much like the world-class athlete must.

Lesson Reminders

- ❖ A contortion is any move away from your gifted self. You will recognize and intuitively know you are in a state of contortion by feelings of uncertainty and thoughts of confusion or anger. Contorting is becoming someone you are not meant to be by nature, where your gifts are hidden or overlooked. There will always be these times of contortion. Each one is its own learning lesson and is meant to strengthen your sense of self and the use of your gifts.

- ❖ People contort in all kinds of life situations. Children first learn about contortion when they interact with peers or enter formalized group settings, such as a school classroom. In these settings, the child begins to speak differently, express values not their own, adapt their hobbies, and they might change their social circles. Contortion may start during the formative years and can have long-term consequences.

- ❖ Athletes share the experience of contortion with professionals from all kinds of work environments, including yours. When athletes undergo contortion, they forget about how to express their gifts. Similarly, you can recall an experience of contortion in your workplace, when you were not the very best version of yourself. Although you certainly experienced the losses from your contortion, so too did your workplace. Your gifts were a large part of the reason why you were hired. When you contorted, you stopped sharing those gifts with others and there was a loss to the giftedness of the organization. Never assume your contortion is a personal loss alone.

❖ Follow a systematic series of steps when you have experienced a contortion. The learning process is referred to as debriefing. You begin to debrief by examining your role in your contortion experience. Understand not only that the contortion happened but also how it started and why it continued. Examining your accountability is a necessary first part of debriefing. You can also benefit from trusted friends to help you examine the contortion experience. By the end of the debriefing process, you will have learned more about your gifts, how easy it is to abandon them, and most important, that you can return to your giftedness any time you choose.

THE SOCIAL SCIENTIST

The young professional—a former equestrian and student—began his dream job as a university professor. He had envisioned this career for many years while he was an athlete, student, and postgraduate, before finally being hired. Even with a newly secured professor's job, his path forward remained uncertain—there was not yet tangible proof the new hire could become creative in this new environment. Could he become an international-level educator at an equivalent or higher level than who and what he formerly was as an athlete? He loved and respected his colleagues; they were welcoming, social, and intently focused on being teachers who were readily available to their students. Although he loved to teach, he was equally an aspiring social scientist and supporter of world-class athletes. Could he launch into this new, exciting, and yet exacting world without losing who he was? To avoid being classified with the status quo of teaching and contributing to university committees as a confined career path, he needed to gain research funding. The present needs left the young professor feeling desperate, ready to grasp at straws. Should he add a new twist to someone else's existing ideas? However, he also envisioned being recognized internationally as an evidence-based scholar and practitioner to elite performers, just as he promised during the recent job interview. He was compelled to make good on his promises, to quickly conceive a research topic, and then to develop a research funding application to establish prominence in the workplace.

After one generic day of teaching and meeting with colleagues, with a tired and yet desperate mind, he went for a walk with his spouse, who was his best friend, and their dogs. They wandered through the expansive woods and wilderness where they lived—a place filled with wildlife. The young couple discussed the life experiences he brought to his university job and how these could be developed into something meaningful and innovative. One idea resonated based on a recent experience as a motivational consultant. In one of the sports he was involved with as a consultant, there were many culturally diverse athletes. Some of the indigenous athletes would join the elite sport organization and soon after return to their cultural communities and forgo their athletic dreams of becoming the world's best. The athletes often ate on their own during team meals and sat in solitude during the long, slow gaps of time between training, meals, and rest, their eyes and bodies averted from the group. These athletes did not feel a sense of belonging in their sport, even though being part of their team was necessary if they were to endure and become world-class performers, something well within reach. Their visible loneliness and impeded pursuits were troubling, yet no one seemed to notice the athletes' emotional distress and rapid departures from the team. The departing athletes and those in the organization shared a mutual sense of loss, with missed opportunities for friendships and excellence.

During the insightful walk in the woods, the young professor began to envision a research idea. He knew the indigenous athletes felt, and in fact were, excluded. What he failed to understand was why they were lonely and separated from teammates and staff. He suspected that the athletes were experiencing culturally unfamiliar and insensitive practices from staff and teammates. Similarly, he observed that teammates and staff rarely sought to understand the solitary athletes, affirming a lack of effort and interest. Over the subsequent weeks and months, the professor began speaking with local indigenous community leaders about his observations and asked for their help and partnership in resolving the cultural divide. Every athlete deserved the opportunity to live authentically while being supported in their rightful paths to world-class status. The community members cautiously agreed to help with the project, but they lacked trust and understanding of how their time and effort would benefit local indigenous athletes. They had already walked similar paths in their youth as sport participants or witnessed them as adults.

Early the following spring, the professor and the project team were awarded research funding to explore the practical barriers experienced by aspiring indigenous elite athletes. Within two weeks of being awarded the money, the professor was invited to attend a meeting in the local indigenous community and present the project once more. He traveled alone to meet the community's elders and leadership. The meeting took place in a beautifully furnished large room, with open ceilings, wood beams, and windows the size of walls. The sun shone into the room, its brightness illuminating a large circle of elders and the community's chief, who sat the farthest from the young professional's assigned chair. A short prayer was said in the local indigenous language, followed by the ceremonial burning of sage. The process unfolding was foreign to the professor, who had been taught to lead and not follow in research. He wondered whether his present moment of uncertainty could be compared to the uncertainty experienced by the indigenous athletes who also were expected to participate in unfamiliar processes. He was about to learn a considerable amount about himself and the people he would work with for many years to come. The chief spoke first and offered a gracious welcome. The people in the circle sat silent as he asked a defining question to the visitor of European ancestry. The question was simple and yet it struck at the foundation of the partnership to come. The chief asked, "Who are you?"

Every young adult beginning a new chapter in life searches the soul to define that very question. The young professor's initial answer included what he was, meaning his station in life, consisting of a doctorate and university professor's position; these were previous glimpses, now captured. The chief, wise and foreseeing a teachable moment for the visitor, stated that qualifications do not reveal who one *is*, only what one does. The young professor quickly realized he was being asked to dig a little deeper into his own truthfulness. How he defined himself would give the community a clearer picture of whether they could work with him. He took a deep breath and approached the question again, this time based on where he came from, meaning his life path. He explained his Eastern European descent and some of the associated struggles his grandparents experienced fleeing to North America. He then narrowed further to his childhood experience, in which he and his sister were the only two children of a certain ethnicity in a rural elementary school, where they were ostracized by peers and he was bullied at a young age. He then spoke about the young indigenous athletes he first met as a professional, many of whom felt separate from their teammates because of their racial identities, and how troubling the pattern was for the athletes and the broader system. Those in attendance listened intently but feared further injury from a foreigner who was asking them to spend their time, effort, and knowledge on a path incompatible with their cultural ways.

Those in the group began to share their experiences, and the young professor glimpsed his future. His work needed to be built from relationships with people; it needed to model those relationships; and the work needed to be guided by meaning and with care. Research was the starting point to a healthy cultural exchange and the forging of a strong kinship, but it took on a unique shape different from any that the team members anticipated. The group worked closely over a decade and became known internationally for their research and even more well known as people who overcame historical differences and harm. For the young professor, the experience further defined how he was to engage in research, teaching, and work with young elite athletes. He better understood the importance of respect for diversity and the paths people should be free to walk, paths equally diverse and perhaps more challenging than his own.

It is easy to confuse what we do with who we are, now more so than ever before. Perhaps the reason for this tendency is the daily investment in our activities, such as sports, work, and training. Activities can easily become part of a broader human identity, just as researchers have found that people can have an athletic, a workplace, and a family identity. However, when you dig a little deeper into who you are, as the chief asked me to do, you will discover a history, values, and a network of social relationships that also define you. These more personal aspects in your life transcend any stage of your development; in fact, they extend across a lifetime, unlike an activity-based identity.

One of many lessons to be gained from this story, beyond learning to be sensitive toward others, is that we can easily fall into the trap of identifying ourselves based on our activities (what we do) as opposed to the deeper parts of who we really are, which in turn we should bring to bear into the various activities in our lives. Each day, challenge yourself to look beyond what you are doing to your deeper personhood and the meaning behind your choices as you tap into your gifts.

LESSON FOUR
GLIMPSES

> *When you catch a glimpse of your potential, that's when passion is born.*
>
> Zig Ziglar

Intuition is an essential human quality when it comes to rediscovering your gifts. In relation to this lesson, intuition encourages you to become aware of more possibilities to thrive in your life. You might listen to or ignore that fleeting but familiar internal call to tap into a potential gift when it comes to your attention. You might see or read about someone else engaging in an activity that was previously your thing or an activity that matches one of your past or present gifts. Sometimes your mind will wander (at least for fleeting seconds) to potential moments of fun and engagement with these potential gifts—your hidden treasures. For a little while you might overlook a gift and the promise of an even better, more complete you. Forgetting these glimpses into your gifts is never permanent unless you continue to force them back down to the depths of your awareness through inattention or because of other priorities. Glimpses of hidden gifts can remain covered where there is no chance for you to inspect and engage with them. We all have ignored many glimpses in our lifetime. The question is not whether glimpses will return to you, but whether you are ready to catch them when they do return and then do the best possible thing: act! This lesson is about the importance of glimpses and the power of their recognition as part of your forward journey to using as many gifts as you dare.

My favorite movie about glimpses is *The Family Man* (28). The story is about a wealthy businessman who thinks he has everything. One day he expresses to an angel disguised as someone in financial need that he wishes for nothing more than his current high-powered job, worldly possessions, and privileged state of being. It is then his story begins to unravel. He goes to sleep one night and wakes up, much to his surprise, next to his old sweetheart—a woman he had loved and let go of for the self-centered pursuit of a career—and to two disheveled children, one requiring a diaper change, the other wanting him to produce breakfast. He lives in a much more modest suburban house and works for his father-in-law managing a tire store. Yet he discovers in this simplified, odd life that he now has more friends, a kinship with his neighbors, and finds happiness being with people and enjoying a meal, a beverage, a cigar, bowling, and the fun of belonging to a local suburban community. When he awakens from the dream to his life of wealth and solitude, he realizes that despite his professional standing he is desperately lonely; his life feels incomplete and of little substantive worth. As the movie transitions to the hope of a happy conclusion, he recognizes he is the most gifted and best version of himself as an engaged partner and parent, living among family and friends, and he chases down his long-lost love and desperately tries to help her recognize the glimpse he experienced in his dream. The glimpse presented in this film is all about reconnecting with yourself and your long-lost passions and a potential return to and avid pursuit of them.

The idea of discussing glimpses is important in relation to you becoming a fuller version of who you can be, with more of your gifts front and center in your daily life. The concept is simple: The more of your gifts you draw upon, the more complete will be your engagement and fulfillment with the world around you. So, how did we arrive at a discussion about glimpses? In lesson one we considered your wonderful innate gifts. For lesson two, we looked at the importance of dueling forces, those times when you feel like you are being pulled in two opposing directions. These forces were described as counters to one another. The existence of competing forces in your life can be healthy if they remind you to choose one of your gifts rather than to choose an activity that is counterintuitive to your path forward. For example, if your gift is teaching or any related skill where you are on the front lines contributing to the positive development of other people, then the desire to teach and nurture might be a force coming from one direction. Its opposing force might be administrative tasks, such as paperwork, that take you into a back room and away from the people you really want to work with and support right now. The logical choice in this scenario is to prioritize activities where you can mentor and to ask others more interested in administrative tasks to take on skills that play to their strengths. Trouble happens when a force pulls you away from your best version of yourself and your gift is sidelined. Part of you is then hidden and altered, leading to a feeling of incompleteness in your daily life and potentially in your longer-term life path. You then risk becoming contorted, the topic covered in lesson three. Contortions happen when you give in to a competing force, such as demands that block the time originally set aside to nurture that special gift of yours, and you replace time spent using your gifts with busywork. The personal result of contorting will be sadness, anger, and dissatisfaction if you stop and analyze how you feel. These imbalances will seep into your approach to daily life, creating less-than-optimal engagement and value. If glimpses are always at the edge of your awareness, recognize each one as it briefly comes to your attention with a fleeting sense of "this is how I should be living my life." Glimpses are intended to be your mind's eye offering an antidote to choices that have taken you away from your gifts.

Your Environment and the Innate You

I used to willingly believe that people reflect their current selves because of social learning and environmental influences. A large body of scientific knowledge about the importance of social learning traces back to discussions from more than 50 years ago (29). Environments strongly influence the shaping of personal behaviors, such as how you choose to engage in your career and the way you relate with others, such as coworkers. Most important, you will learn from the influence of others whether to bring your gifts to the forefront in a specific part of your life. I have written about an approach to performance in which I point out that people are influenced by their contexts in terms of the practices they must adopt to get along and work effectively (30). Behaviors like being formal and inhibited might be regarded as necessary organizational practices (for example, in some highly formal workplaces or social groups), but they can and will also block your version of giftedness.

However, I believe that no matter how important environments are in teaching you how to effectively navigate your day given the people and situations you face, glimpses of who you really are and what you can bring to the table will always exist inside of you because they are a central part of your unique approach to life. Glimpses help you remain resilient to counterforces and the mistaken paths you might find yourself on when contortion is part of your current state of living. Many athletes and employees suffer because they are masking their gifts. Consider a person with a bohemian and fun approach to learning and mastering their professional craft alongside others. This one person could be a ray of sunshine for everyone they touch. Such a person, when not allowed to express their fun approach, may contort into a sad version of the performer they once were—someone who enjoyed doing what they were gifted to do and whose performances were like watching the uninhibited dancer let loose on the dance floor. What have you witnessed at childhood school dances and adult dances alike? As soon as a single person begins to dance, the power of that individual becomes a positive gravitational force attracting positivity in those nearby. The dance floor fills, and everyone begins to dance; all that is needed is one person and that person's courage to share their love of movement. Almost every supreme athlete I have met experiences glimpses in their careers that can help pull them onto (or back onto) their path. These glimpses help inspire the athletes from an unawareness of a much needed and perhaps forgotten gift to the awareness of a part of themselves that needs to be opened or reopened, prepared, and put into action so that the gift can be used while it is of personal benefit. This sequence has been borrowed from scholars fascinated by how people's behaviors can change and become their new normal (31); and it has been applied by motivational consultants and clinicians to support motivational increases through a series of interviewing steps, thereby helping people make positive life changes (32).

Some years ago, a friend asked me to work with a client who was clearly at an athletic career crossroad. The athlete was accomplished at the international level but had yet to reach their version of complete performer and achieve world-class results. As a performer, this athlete was extremely intelligent, had extraordinary stamina, and had deep determination to win but was struggling with their judgment. When the athlete and I spoke for the first time, it was apparent that the athlete had lost all passion for the sport. The athlete's training environment was toxic, and they felt devalued in terms of the personal gifts they held dearly. Their resilience, intelligence, and abundant leadership qualities were being mocked by personal coaches as were the many well-developed athletic gifts bestowed on this client from birth. Their enjoyment of the sport was low, leading them to question whether to continue to devote time and effort or retire from sports and transition to the next stage of life, where their gifts could be applied elsewhere, such as in leadership positions. The athlete then explored what drew them into the sport. In telling of the journey, they experienced a glimpse, a sense of knowing that the best was yet to come in the sport. They still had better versions of performance within them not yet tapped because of inhibition, ones that could bring them to the summit of the sport. The Olympics were also calling; the athlete always wanted to be an Olympian and to perform at the highest level on the highest profile world stage. Following a few discussions, the athlete decided to move from one training environment and coaching staff to a new support system. Their training almost immediately caught fire and they became a much better version of themself, one they always knew existed but had been previously unable to channel given how contorted they felt in the previous training environment. Within the year, this same athlete ranked among the top three in the world, an achievement previously unattained. This same athlete continued along a path of memorable accomplishments, and they continued to glimpse parts of themselves as an athlete that had not yet been willed into existence. Glimpses kept coming, building one on top of the previous one, synergistically. When people are open to their glimpses, they become aware of further opportunities and a healthy direction forward. The story culminated with the athlete not only becoming a world-class success but also becoming someone who continues to serve as an inspirational model of resilience for youth within and beyond sports.

Glimpses of our gifts are visible to anyone watching, beyond ourselves, from the very beginning of our existence to the end of our lives. For example, I witnessed a glimpse early on in one special life and watched how it evolved into something remarkable. When my oldest son was a newborn, a few minutes into his life outside the womb, he lay under the hospital's heat lamps, minutes after birth, examining his hands as if he was finally making sense of the appendages before his eyes. It seemed that his hands were an unformed puzzle he could not make sense of during developmental months within the womb. I watched him move his fingers, never taking his eyes off them, in what appeared to those in the room as a puzzled facial expression. He does his own certain something with his fingers that to the present day stops those of us who were there with him in those first minutes of life dead in our tracks. He wiggles his fingers as if playing the piano. He was very curious of what was in front of him at the beginning of life and remains so to this date. Many years later, as we sit at the dinner table immersed in family conversation or when I wander into his room to play or speak with him, I see his original hand movements played out before my eyes. He is unaware that his unique finger movements have been with him since birth, and so we quietly watch him. As I learn more about my son each day, I have come to realize that as interesting as his finger movements are in and of themselves, what is really fascinating about him is what the hand movements represent. His gift is curiosity and a desire to reach out into the world. He asks so many questions that my wife and I have nicknamed him The Questioner. This very same inquisitive person has progressed rapidly in school and in combative sports because he asks questions of himself and other people. He wants to know about the people in his environment. He stops people—senior citizens in grocery stores, restaurant owners, people going about their day's work—and asks them how they are doing and other unpredictable but well-suited and interesting questions that stop them in their tracks. Lately this has resulted in various businesses trying to recruit him into employment, unsolicited, despite his youth and inexperience. He is interested in people, and he sees the people in front of him as important. Curiosity is his gift, and it has opened his world, just as it has opened the world for us, his parents, and for his close friends and the teammates he trains with each week in his karate dojo. The gift of curiosity and the natural inclination to express it to others is his gift, leaving my son highly relational.

Tuning In to Your Gifts

Every person who is tuned in experiences glimpses regularly, just as each person can witness glimpses of gifts in a child or an aspiring elite athlete. The key is to remain tuned in to our own gifts as well as the gifts of others when they surface in the form of glimpses. I experienced a life-altering glimpse that changed the course of my life, and I share my story to spur your thoughts toward your own life-altering glimpse. Sometimes glimpses come out of thin air, but often they are ignited through experiences, such as listening to music, or in my case, through running while listening to music. The activities themselves put me in the frame of mind to listen for a glimpse.

Many years ago, I was an athletic, agile endurance athlete with stamina and spark. Little by little, I neglected this treasured part of my person as I chased my academic career and consulting opportunities. I became less of an endurance athlete to the point that I almost forgot I was one. I was compromised in strength, stamina, physical health, and life balance. I accepted my decline in physical fitness as a sign of aging, much like a green leaf eventually turns color in autumn, falls from the tree, and disintegrates to compost. The clear imbalance in my life was caused by my allowance of forces that pulled me away from my athletic gifts. The imbalance was too much scientific and applied hours at the expense of my own well-being. In 2014, my life changed dramatically because of a glimpse. I experienced a profound recognition while trying to do a slow run with a national team coach and the team's athletic trainer, who were good friends. We were at an international sport event and wanted to get out of doors and take some time away from the athletes we were supporting and to exert ourselves through some physical activity. We stepped outside and basked in the late spring sunshine as we prepared for a slow run. My friends stretched their limbs methodically as the physically active often do, and I faked my way through what I thought was a warming process in the eyes of my friends. We then began our run, a proposed distance of about four miles (about 6 km). Before long, I was winded and lagging. Even the short distance I asked of my mind and body was at that moment out of my reach. My two running mates, neither of whom were in their youth either, were fitter athletes. They slowed down and waited, though not before teasing me about my lack of stamina and toughness. We finished prematurely at a walk. They did not want to leave me, their deflated and relieved teammate, behind. In that very moment I was undergoing a glimpse—I was at a physical crossroad. My fitness and youthfulness—an important part of who I once was—had been replaced. I, who had once been a talented endurance athlete, was nearly 40 pounds overweight with faltering cardiovascular fitness, poor eating habits, and poor life balance. I was supposed to be a credible mental performance coach to world-class athletes. How could I possibly inspire fit, committed athletes and seem creditable to their coaches given my self-neglect and what it said of my own life choice of moving away from the world of sport and being physically tough? I was no longer wise to what it felt like to push a body—my body—to its limits through pain and to success. The athletes likely thought I knew what it meant theoretically to endure through exertion to exhaustion and beyond, that place where a person really knows oneself. Knowing intimately by living the experience of physical stamina and sheer will is a requirement of my job; this is what I attempt to impart to clients and to those who only daydream of working with the very best of performers. There will always be a distinction between knowing excellence at a theoretical level and knowing it first-hand.

To excel in anything, a person needs to understand how to journey to the bottom of themselves and how to systematically stretch their endurance, whether it is physical, mental, emotional, or all of these at once, to their self-imposed limits and beyond. Pushing oneself to personal limits must be personally known before preaching the same lesson to someone else on their quest toward excellence. To reach the redline means reaching deep inside yourself to the essence of who you are and working through the physical, emotional, or mental equivalent of a dark tunnel to push the limits of your capabilities. In my case the inner athlete had been hibernating, much like a bear in winter holed up in a dark den. I could either continue with my inactive life and an unfit body or I could alter my path and choose an improved and once familiar lifestyle with self-care and a reboot of temporarily concealed physical abilities. On that day I glimpsed a distant gift I wanted to channel again out of necessity. Through my glimpse experience I recognized my crossroad: either go back to my current lifestyle and forget all about the fascinating run experience or make a dramatic shift in terms of fitting up and eating more carefully. The benefit would be a return to my athletic gift of endurance sports. I chose the second option—immediate action based on my glimpse—and on that day I became an athlete once more.

For months I took solitary daily runs during which I struggled before rediscovering my footing. Solitary runs were a safe reengagement with my gift because I had to stop for walks along the way, recover, and then continue. Those first few runs were painful, but over time, physical pain and frustration with my body were replaced with energy and enthusiasm and then with a pledge to continue my path. At the next athlete training camp,

I was ready. I ran on a track with the same coaches, one being a marathon runner, and to my amazement we all kept the same pace. Within the same year, I began to accompany professional athletes on their long runs in high-altitude training camps where I ran side-by-side with athletes and their coaching staff, no longer lagging. As my fitness began to surpass coaches and team staff, some of whom were recognizably hibernating from their physical care, I was sent onto the roads to spend time with the athletes. Only I could keep up and track their roadwork and exertion while supporting their efforts. I also learned more about the athletes as we ran side-by-side, up and down mountains, in sleet, hail, sunshine, extreme cold, and extreme heat. The following year, I entered my first of many half marathons and ran 1:45, a modest time. The experience was defining and reignited a spark to run and to compete; the spark became a very small flame, followed by combustion and a return to a few natural gifts from my youth tied to my athletic identity. Since then, I have road and trail raced in many events and now run well below 90 minutes for a half marathon, always pushing my boundaries beyond earlier times. My athletic body is much older, but I recognize it as a seasoned and hardened version of its original form rather than a wilting leaf past its summer season. I am again able to relive the gift of physical stamina and ease of movement. I revel in the temporary pain of exertion and the enduring experience of physical success as I have returned to the world of sports competition, this time on the front lines. Running is the newfound expression of my athletic self, an identity alive and well, reignited from what could otherwise have been a fleeting moment of sad recognition, acceptance, further physical decline, and unhappiness with my body and my life balance.

Glimpses can become life-altering realities. These realities can add to the quality of each day in terms of physical, emotional, and psychological well-being. Scholars argue that good and bad habits take months to begin and years to develop (33), but my path to change began immediately out of a desperate recognition of necessity. The glimpse of my inactive previous self remains a reminder of a poor series of decisions, resulting in a poor habit and pathway that, for me, once was and can once again become an easy unhealthy default. Sometimes I hear someone suggest I am overzealous in my sports activities and that I am pushing myself too hard for my age. Even colleagues from my own field have shared this view with me. I like what my reinvigorated body can do and who I represent; so, I scoff at any remarks directed at my running habits and continue happily on my path, tapping into my gift of endurance. You also will experience glimpses, and I hope you also will act on yours. When you act on your glimpses, be prepared that not everyone will support the improved you. Some people will be supportive and excited for you and others less so. Acting on your gifts might make some people feel uncomfortable with their own inactivity and stalled development. Why? Because everyone is on their own path toward and away from personal gifts. People who are pursuing their giftedness will be more likely to understand and support your glimpses and readiness to thrive as you will support theirs. You will also encounter people who are struggling with competing forces or who are in a state of contortion. For these people, witnessing the potential progression of someone else—you, even if you are friends—might become a source of frustration and cause tension in your relationship. The person contorting has the power to channel their frustration and tap into it as a starting point in the exploration and glimpsing of their own gifts. How a person reacts to another person's positive traction toward gifts is their choice. Regardless, you must act on your glimpses of the gifts you hold and stay the course, choosing to chase them down or risk your version of sustained hibernation.

Many people say they are too busy to read or even to think, let alone to do something healthy and reinforce their gifts. I hear daily from people who claim they are overextended and confined to or trapped in a rigid and fixed schedule, without time for their version of play and self-care. They believe their life situation is astronomically different and more demanding than the lives of the vibrant people they encounter, which is a falsehood. Working feverishly, though perhaps not wisely, becomes the rationalization and crutch causing people to limp along through unsatisfying life paths—even people in professions associated with mental health and motivation. They know what they should do, but they are not doing what they should. And so, I regularly hear excuses from colleagues worldwide, from scientists and people on the front lines working with athletes and sport organizations. At times I challenge my colleagues who are friends when they draw on excuses at the expense of their health and balance. There is certainly nothing wrong and everything right with putting one's nose to the grindstone when it comes time to focus on work. But there must also be time each day for rejuvenation and self-reflection about whether you have worked with your gifts to their best advantage. Only in moments of stillness and moments away from the shackles of daily commitments can you rediscover your gifts and where and how you can use them as often as possible. Glimpses happen quickly, but they only resonate when you permit yourself the opportunity to recognize the messages and intuition signaling from within, much like a beacon from a distant lighthouse. Every elite performer arrives at a juncture in their career, whether it is professional or personal, foreseeable, or not. Where the most successful athletes see their opportunities and resources and opt for the best versions of themselves, others only see problems and then try to impose barriers, blockades, and resistance to the one trying to be authentic and do what they are meant to. Energy and time are spent looking for and investing in rich personal resources as opposed to seeking help supportive of progression. Your glimpses are signposts you have identified at some level of recognition. You have free will to forge ahead and pursue excellence or to deviate and digress. But when the glimpse is lost, the immediate opportunity to excel and become your best version of selfhood is lost too.

Action Item Four: Recognize, Envision, and Document Your Glimpses

Glimpses, along with following the pathways through competing forces and personal contortions, are common experiences across people. You are aware of this process and are highly self-aware, having completed action items one through three. You've had many glimpses over the course of your life, one building onto the next. They began in childhood when you might have just known you were meant to do something—the boxer decides to box; the footballer decides to play football; and the guitar player picks up the guitar for the first time, simply knowing they are meant to be a rock star. You have stumbled onto many realizations of something or someone who could help improve your life. Similarly, in this lesson I told about a special quality I glimpsed in my son, and then I described my own glimpsing experience when I was faltering during a run with my teammates. I fell short and considered my status at that very moment as compared to the physically endurant athlete I once was. As saddened as I was because of the stamina I no longer had, I was equally frustrated with the moment I was in and why I was there, which spurred personal change. My glimpse was the contrast of my gift compared with my current state. The glimpse spurred emotions—partly frustration, partly hope. You've had similar glimpses, and perhaps like many people you paid little attention to them other than moments of fleeting reminiscence about a time or a version of yourself passed and irretrievable. You might have been frustrated by your glimpse, turning it away and dismissing the opportunity before you. Another glimpse was then lost to the recesses of your memory and shelved, where the glimpse, like a book, continued to gather dust. Perhaps your glimpse was yet another on a pile of recurring glimpses, and you said, "I really ought to be making this change."

Now is the time to catch your glimpses by first recognizing the next glimpse when it taps you on the shoulder. When you experience your next glimpse, recognize that it is happening and at the first possible convenience, write down what the glimpse was, when it occurred, and how it came to be. Did the glimpse surface out of nowhere, or was there something or someone who helped you with your experience of déjà vu? Next, consider what the glimpse means to you right now. Instead of asking yourself whether you can set aside time to revisit the glimpse, set aside the time as soon as possible that day, without excuse, and reexamine your glimpse. Set aside time for yourself, where you can explore a special and once familiar gift, now hidden, and its potential application. This is a necessary part of how you will refine yourself and continue to grow as opposed to being stuck in your current stagnate state. The contradiction to what I suggest is a life with limited imagination and opportunity that often leads to personal crisis and poor life quality that affects yourself and everyone around you. People have an amazing ability to change what they are doing, to alter their life course, and to plan a new and improved return to happiness and balance. Your return to your right path might be found in a hobby, a job change, or a different peer group. These improvements to your life, assuming they serve as resurfacing agents, can assure better quality of life and happiness, reinvigorate you, and help you think with more wisdom.

I encourage athletes who struggle with their life paths by not paying attention to their glimpses to engage in a visioning of their future life at its best through various exercises, some in the mind, some more concrete and lingering. A vision board is one exercise for the person who likes to consider their best version of life as having different elements. Vision boards require a large, plain cardboard poster. Then you search magazines and websites of all sorts and identify potential aspects of your life that you want to explore and develop. The ideas and concepts might include something you've held relating to a sports-related gift or any other gift that has been waiting in the background. The sport or physical activity is a gift that is meant for leisure time. Other elements you can add might include the sort of living accommodation you desire, such as wooded land or an urban lot, or a location where you can tap into another gift such as becoming an amateur farmer. You can then add in the elements of your ideal workplace, perhaps an environment that pulls out your interpersonal and leadership skills. The board could further extend to the sorts of interpersonal relationships that would fan your flame, perhaps through pictures of friends connecting over social gatherings outdoors and through meals around a nice table with family. Your choice of integrated images should be considered in terms of how they will help you channel the most diversely gifted version of yourself. Vision boards are then mounted on a kitchen or bedroom wall and reviewed each morning as you start the day, over your morning meal.

If you really enjoy art and coloring, you could also use a mandala drawing. This circular drawing is a broad glimpse into your potential improved future as opposed to glimpsing one activity or pursuit in isolation. It is much like the vision board, although one glimpsed image dominates. I have used this same exercise before interviewing many Olympic and professional athletes to really help them understand and put their thoughts into words (34). The mandala drawing is one you create by drawing a circle. Your circle will symbolize a 360-degree vision of where you wish to be (in a nutshell), what you wish to do, how you wish to do it, who you wish to include, and the sorts of lifestyle decisions you want to add into your day to improve life balance.

So how do you draw a mandala? Draw a circle. Begin anywhere you wish in the circle and go from there. You can use colored pencils, and then with an open mind, write words and draw images. Some people begin in the center, others at the top, some work from right to left, and so on. Let your mind flow and slowly but surely build your full scope of vision a little bit at a time. I have seen mandalas from athletes drawn with a podium at its apex; the athlete somewhere near the center of the drawing; a national flag placed somewhere; their relationships, perhaps beneath their athletic image, propping them up; and various other interests placed somewhere along the periphery, such as education, other hobbies, and a job. Before long, you will have all these related meaningful images, some in vibrant colors and others in tranquil colors. Some of the accompanying words might be written at the center of your circle, whereas others might be placed on the periphery. Once you are finished with your drawing, look at it. Present it to a close trusted friend or family member to gain more insight into your glimpse. The mandala drawing, like the vision board, is then to be posted in a frequently visited location in your house, maybe with a copy at your work desk, so you can return to it many times each day and enjoy what you are planning next in your exciting life.

A further addition to your daily regimen is to keep a small pocket pad or use your mobile device to immediately record any glimpse as it happens. Upon documenting the glimpse, text it as a message to yourself so you are certain to keep the idea in the forefront of your mind once the initial thought has passed. When you return home at the end of your day, revisit your text or note and begin to expand on what the glimpse could become in fullest Technicolor, assuming you choose to pursue it, which constitutes a deliberate choice on your part. From its earliest inception, you should always regard each documented glimpse as dynamic. Glimpses must be enriched, because ideas surrounding the initial glimpse will layer in with the fullness of time. Add new insights to your vision board or mandala drawing. Most every great creation begins as a glimpse, which then becomes the launching pad to a grander idea, followed by reality. In my earliest discussion walking in the woods with my partner, we discussed ideas about the importance of working with indigenous elite athletes and developing a research project to drive future supportive interventions for Olympic teams. The glimpse became a research project, which then developed into a series of publications and interventions, and later into a globally recognized line of practice focused on the cultural inclusiveness of marginalized clients (35). Every glimpse is its own pearl of wisdom, first captured as a grain of sand and then grown until it becomes a highly valued tangible part of your existence. However, I offer one caution: Don't attempt to plot too much of your inner vision (through drawing or boarding) all at once. Such an overcommitment could only lead to discouragement and disillusionment. Your progress in the quest of your vision will only be gained one step at a time and one glimpse at a time, with persistent shaping and reshaping of your developing life.

⏰ Lesson Reminders

- ❖ Glimpses are fleeting internal reminders of how you can further develop yourself, maybe exploring a new application of an old gift. They are meant to stir hope in you and help you add an aspect to your life that plays to your existing gifts or some new possibility. A glimpse experience is instinctive but might be stimulated by a visual reminder, something told to you, or something you witness that opens the possibility of engagement with one of your gifts. No matter how your glimpse is encountered, it is a call from within for positive action.

- ❖ Glimpses are common experiences to every person. Yet most people dismiss their glimpses or fail to recognize them due to a busy schedule and a lack of attention to what our mind and soul are tell us. Ignoring your glimpses is inefficient and serves as a counterforce to the nurturance of your exquisite gifts. Your job is to recognize and take note of your glimpses when they happen so they are not lost, only to be experienced again later. Noting your glimpses requires you to use your handheld device or piece of paper and record the glimpse as soon as you experience it.

- ❖ Continue to shape your glimpses after they are first experienced. A glimpse is only the first step in your positive life change. Once you've experienced the glimpse and taken note of it, plan how to press the glimpse into action. The action step must be planned out before you act. Once you put your glimpse into action, be patient with yourself because changes of habit and refinements in life take time to establish. Little by little, with persistence, your glimpse will become a full-blown gift and part of your new normal.

- ❖ Once you start to recognize and act on your glimpses, you are going to become more aware of new ones when they happen. Having one glimpse is only the beginning of your journey. One glimpse could lead to a new glimpse or the evolution of a recent one, just as my glimpse to run led to competitive endurance running. The glimpsing process never stops with a single glimpse that you are now hooked to. Develop more than one gift. The more multidimensional you are because of fostering the application of gifts, the fuller life becomes. When you develop several gifts, they should reflect a healthy balance in your daily life. So, one glimpse might be in relation to work or school, a second to personal life, and a third to a recreational activity.

LESSON FIVE

ENDURANCE

> *The will to win, the desire to succeed, the urge to reach your full potential . . . These are the keys that will unlock the door to personal excellence.*
>
> Confucius

The idea sewn throughout this book is that you must embrace the gifts you were born with, including the qualities you rediscover through your glimpses, despite the internal or external forces that can potentially take you in an undesired direction. The consequences of doing and being someone other than who you are slows your potential. We began this journey with a story about a headstrong horse, uniquely and unrelentingly herself. Barriers never held the horse back regardless of whether they were fences or misinformed human will, both of which could have easily gated her in by blocking her gifts, career progression, and a deeper application of her personality. The horse undertook actions aligned with what could be interpreted as glimpses of her own greatness as a running and jumping prodigy. Her decisions were instinctive, likely without foresight of where they would lead her. She was playing to her gifts each time she bounded over yet another fenced-in area; through her jumping antics, she let others know exactly what her gifts were. The horse was looking to enjoy her gifts instead of pleasing people. By attempting to please others, we sometimes please no one, least of all ourselves. She then endured on a path aligned with her skills by jumping over the fences in her way. In so doing, she was dismissive of her counterforce—that is, living out an existence without jumping and galloping. She then became an international competitor in a relatively short time and was recognized within the horse world as having met a standard of being among the elite.

I often marvel how my former equine partner and friend could just as easily have been misdirected onto an inauthentic path had she chosen not to remain herself. Consequently, she was granted the opportunity of rehoming and finding people who understood and placed value in her gifts and her spirit.

Remember the initial purchaser, a renowned horse trader, was able to place value in certain horse stock but could not see the horse's true qualities because these were unfamiliar or of little worth to her new owner. Like my spirited and unrelenting horse, you must exercise free will to choose your own path and then prepare to walk or run forward to your dreams. Everyone must do the same thing or suffer their own inertia. Once you choose to act, your effort is going to become somewhat repetitive in terms of your daily commitment to practice. The recreational runner, for example, trains to eventually become a marathoner, a skill that can only be honed with time, patience, and a systematic approach until body and mind are one and this new part of the gifted person is eventually formed. Only then can you move with your gifts beyond their promise to the equivalent of them becoming food for your soul, any time, each day.

Lesson five is focused on the next monumental step needed for you to tap into your gifts. Much like my equine partner and I chose to act on what became our shared glimpse of becoming jumping and galloping machines, you must begin to invest hours of your time, playing with your giftedness so that it becomes a key part of your future existence. When I use a necessary term like *endurance* and its associated academic term of *persistence* (36), I'm referring to your unrelenting pursuit of your gift. Endurance is about putting your nose to the grindstone and persevering with the commitment of time and effort needed to build up your gift to its rightful shape and quality—one you will be proud of.

Artifacts and Self-Affirmations

The ability of human capacity to endure for a long time fascinated me well before I became a social scientist and worked on staff within elite sports. As an aspiring elite athlete, I endured in my training, knowing the hours I invested were going to pay dividends. Sometimes, feeling my anticipated level of excellence in the world of equestrian was all that drove me forward. I vividly recall being a young teenager. In the arena where I trained, my father had fastened our national flag to one wall, just above eye level. He was a first-generation newcomer to the country where he lived, so national flags flew proudly throughout our horse farm. Anyone driving up to the top of our horse farm laneway would see the first of these national flags waving in the wind.

The flags represented for him a fulfilled vision of having made it to a country he had dreamed about in his youth. The relevance of those flags for me was quite different. I sensed that one day I would compete at the international level, where my horses and I would be led into performance arenas behind someone proudly holding my country's flag, with an orchestra playing my national anthem in the background and an audience filling the arena to witness the moment. The image lingered in the recesses of my youthful mind as I rode many different horses around the riding ring, traveling enough mileage in a saddle to crisscross the world many times over. Those memorable flags on my family's property served to inspire me. I imagined myself as a potential representative of my nation, much as the idea of finishing atop the podium has inspired many a young and driven athlete who can hear and even feel their national anthems in their most inspired corners of their imagination long before their success became reality (37). The flag represented a visual **artifact**, which refers to any visual reminder, such as a document, picture, or piece of art used to keep you moving forward to your gift (38). The symbol of a flag, like other motivational artifacts helped keep me on my path of daily endurance as I invested countless hours riding horses, even when the weather was unbearable and my hands froze into solid forms that required minutes of progressively warm water to thaw after I returned to my home in need of relief. By the age of 17 I had the qualification criteria needed to compete at the Junior North and South American Championships (termed the Continental Young Riders Championships) pasted to the inside of my bedroom door. The competition represented in my sport the highest-level event an equestrian from my age group could experience. I would look at both artifacts each day, the qualification criteria where I slept and the national flag where I trained. At the age of 20 I replaced the Continental Young Riders selection criteria with something new and exciting because I had competed in four such events already and been in the top ten twice. My new target was the qualification criteria needed to qualify for the Senior Pan-American Games. The Pan-American Games, like the Asian Games, European Games, African Games, and Commonwealth Games, is a senior multi-sport event that is restricted to North and South American elite athletes. It was the logical next step in my journey—becoming a member of my country's senior national team. These posted reminders helped me endure and secure my spot on the national team the following year, just as they had with the previously posted junior qualification events. Soon afterward, I returned to university and enrolled in a series of courses, including one with a kind English literature professor. The final assignment was to write a critical essay on one of several books we were assigned to read. I recall asking an unusual request of the professor: Could I rewrite the ending to one of the books? I sensed I could write a more compelling conclusion than the author, and in the requesting process and the writing that followed, I glimpsed my love of nonacademic writing. Granted, I did not tap into my glimpse as an author for many years, but it would seem I am living out a previous glimpse right now! I continue to suggest, glimpses might be fleeting during a moment in time, but they can and often will resurface and serve to remind you of an opportunity waiting to be acted upon.

Where my glimpse of becoming an equestrian team member included continuous reminders, my glimpse as an author didn't and was therefore misplaced for far too long. We need visual reminders of where we wish to go, much like the exercise choices on a vision board or mandala from lesson four are needed to keep you on track and in alignment with your glimpse. The artifacts you might use could include a job description you are working toward, with its qualifications listed. Your dream might be to develop your gift working for a progressive company; in such a case, a picture representing the outside or inside of the building or a corporate logo could be useful. You might equally have an adult sports dream that could bring your athleticism to full color once more. For example, one of my clients posted an advertisement from an international ironman triathlon competition that they envisioned competing in the following year. Another client posted a picture of the Boston Marathon. Both clients achieved their qualifications and lived out their pursuits. Once the images are chosen and posted to your walls, they become your daily reminders of where you are going and why you are putting in those long, hard hours investing in a gift that is beginning to grow but not yet bearing fruit. Without reminders of where your gifts will help you travel, you risk losing your way because daily time commitments are without context and vision. Thomas Edison reputedly said, "Genius is one percent inspiration and ninety-nine percent perspiration." Although inspiration is proportionately small to the time invested in the pursuit of a gift, it becomes the seasoning in your recipe for success, providing flavor to the anticipated dish you will consume.

Complementing your artifacts, another strategy I use with performers is called self-affirmations (39). A self-affirmation is a statement that reminds you exactly who you intend to be, written as if you are already that person and the statement your reality. The year before the Olympics, an aspiring Olympian will declare (affirm) themselves in the following way: "I am a (year provided) Olympian." What is the purpose of self-affirmations? Affirmations work like artifacts; they are the regular visual reminders developed to keep you focused on your gifts. Affirmations are different from artifacts but even more frequently visible. Affirmations are meant to be placed all over the locations you live in and walk by each day, such as your bedroom, refrigerator, washroom mirror, work desk, and so on. Use vibrant, colorful index cards—bright yellow, pink, and orange—because these colors will capture your eye, making it impossible to ignore them when you walk by. For the exercise to work best there should be three or four important self-affirmations relating to you living with the gift you're pursuing. I suggest that at least a two or three of the four affirmations be focused on you living out the process of being gifted. The final one can be a monumental result-oriented affirmation. The affirmations cards, like all ideas reinforcing the emergence of your gifts, need to be carefully worded, with particular emphasis on skills and processes requiring your attention and time investment.

So how should you begin? Take a second and consider exactly which gift you are choosing to focus on. If you have read this far in the book, you should know the gift by this point. Perhaps your gift is that you are a bright-minded person and want to become a teacher—your dream job. Teaching has always come naturally to you. You are one of those special people who, from early childhood, could easily get your ideas across, for example, to primary grade children. Children of this age group naturally gravitated toward you and followed you around as if you were the pied piper. You love social studies because you feel a connection with the world around you, and you are interested in past and current events happening worldwide. Declare yourself an accredited teacher, meaning you begin to see yourself as having your education degree and teacher's certificate. Therefore, at the bottom of the index card, as your final affirmation, write in your own handwriting, "I am a world-class (whichever grade you choose) social studies primary school teacher." Then put the start date. Next, work backward from the outcome goal you just penned to the gifted parts of yourself as that teacher you just know you will become. Be as precise as possible in developing each aspect. If one of the core elements to being that gifted teacher is really engaging students on world affairs and opening their minds to the large world before them, then be specific about what that learned world-class version of you would look and feel like. You might say: "I am so engaging a teacher of world affairs that my students feel they are world travelers when in my class." A second core element to your giftedness and part of you as the incredible teacher might be your kindness. So write a self-affirmation that speaks to how you relate with your class of inspired children so that they feel fully accepted and loved in your class, to the point that they don't want the class to end. Once you have crafted your affirmations, read them and make certain that the ideas and the language used to present each affirmation reach to the depth of your emotions, such that you are able to say to yourself, "Yes, this is exactly me as I see myself."

The procedural part of this exercise is where you post these around the house. Promise yourself to finish this exercise within the next day. I worked with one national sports team in the weeks before we departed for their world championship. All the athletes did the exercise just described and declared out what they wanted from their sport event. The evening after we did the exercise, the coaches and I were walking by the athletes' rooms on the way to our own. We discovered that only one athlete had posted the self-affirmations on the outside of her door so that she and everyone else could see her declaration. She pledged she was going to be world champion in big letters, followed by the artful creation of her national flag. Nine of the 11 athletes won medals, but there was only one gold medalist. Can you guess who it was? Once the goals are posted all over your daily spaces, you must then contract with yourself to stop and read them each time you walk past each of the index cards. By doing so you will begin to affirm your positive ideas of who you wish to be more frequently than you could have without the cards, likely more than 30 times each day. Compare the high number of reminders you now have in relation to your gifts as compared to how many you had before to reinforce your glimpse. Once you have stopped and read the cards for at least three weeks, all you will need to do is see the color card and touch it to automatically be reminded of your gift and where you are going to apply it. Work with your affirmation cards for at least six weeks, and if you feel any further refinements are needed in relation to your affirmations, then make them and immediately post your cards once more. This is what I refer to as a live exercise, like the artifacts, vision board, and mandala are. Each one needs to be shaped and it needs to reflect the forward evolution in your thinking, doing, and your continued dreaming about what comes next.

The Process of Taking Action

Many books have been written about human endurance through trial and error, one quite recently (40). The idea of enduring reminds us of the associated characteristics of mental toughness, grittiness, sheer human will, and all the pieces necessary for a relentless person to be, well, relentless. Moving forward from your glimpse there will be a few different layers to tackle once you begin to mobilize your energies and prepare for action. These layers are progressive, from general to specific, and important in your endurance as you begin to reach for and apply an additional gift. The most basic, foundational layer is the daily work you must invest in developing your new gift. The work ahead extends well beyond the posting of inspirational artifacts. Scientific evidence suggests it is a challenge to act, and it is an equal but different challenge to endure in the pursuit of your gift (41). On the precipice of each new year, people resolve to make positive changes and be the better version of self they always dreamed they could be. You have likely made at least one New Year's resolution in your time. The term *resolution* is for many people a pledge without true intention. The pledge, despite having no structure to support it, such as executional planning, is being expected to lead to immediate action and a better version of you, beginning with the coming year. However, when you are not fully equipped with the necessary tools and understanding to ensure your successful pursuit, there is a high chance you will not endure even if you have written affirmations. Instead, many people in despair default once again to their old behavior: a gift set aside, returned to its dormant state. Do you know someone who decided they want to return to the physically conditioned and athletically gifted body of their youth? Many adults who have gained weight because of sitting in front of a computer, not sticking with a careful diet, or giving up their self-care to care for a family member or nurture a larger family unit desire to recover their physique and shed those unwanted pounds. Imagine you are in a similar situation, maybe not about weight but about something you wish to regroup from, such as compromised heart health. Perhaps you have made your resolution because of an earlier glimpse of your gift, and you are inspired to go to the store, lighten your wallet, and purchase the necessary equipment to relaunch yourself into a sport—an old favorite, running. You then venture to your local store, excited, bubbling with enthusiasm, and feeling like you are on the precipice of an amazing, life-altering change back to a part of you that you really loved. Along comes the sales manager with a welcoming smile. You try on different shoes until you find the perfect pair. Step one—done. Next, you choose this swanky running shirt in a bright color confirming a committed and highly visible you. You are on a roll now and picking up steam. You buy brand name running shorts, running tights, and a gorgeous running jacket with night visibility so you can be free to run any time of day or night. By this point you look like an athlete again. The salesperson then reminds you to buy a few pairs of running socks, a running hat, maybe some running sunglasses, and the list grows to all kinds of seasonal gear. You agree to all these necessities because you are going the distance! You have built up quite a bill, so with a little flush coming to your face you pull out your plastic because the reinvigorating of your old gift is worth the significant investment. You then carry your full bag of gorgeous sports equipment home with a bounce in your step.

At home you bound through the door, cut off all the tags, excitedly get changed, and set off on that first run with your beautiful equipment. You are practically floating over the ground, and you look and feel great, just as you knew you would. Your vision is now reality; you have physical sensation and joy now added to your quest, tangible proof you are on the right track. Day two follows and you still feel pretty good, then day three, and so on. How do you think your story will continue from here? Does anything in this story resemble your own similar experience? The activity might change and sports gear might be replaced with work clothing, but the concept is the same. The story of financial output and initial action, both of which are important to your progress, gets at the essence of what it begins to mean when we discuss the enduring pursuit of a gift. Assuming you stick with your passion once you have acted, it is the consequence of certain strategic actions you have taken to strengthen your will to succeed.

Remember how I drew on artifacts from my training environment and my room to help me endure in my pursuit as a young athlete? Like any aspiring performer chasing down a gift, you can take similar actions. Use the work from your previous lessons, especially by rereading your previous tasks and activities at the end of each lesson. Review these activities every week to build resolve after the initial glitter becomes a little less shiny and as a new positive change becomes part of a regular weekly schedule. Reviewing those activities and placing reminders of your gift on your walls (as you did with your vision board or mandala drawing and your affirmations) will help maintain your engagement. The more artifacts you draw on for inspiration, the more energy you will build while you are in hot pursuit of that gift. You will also need resources outside of yourself, such as positive people who stand behind you as you build endurance and reinforce your inspiration, just as my family supported me when I devoted a year of my lifeblood to this book. Each of my family members, no matter where they were in relation to their own gift discoveries, were constant in their support of my quest of the gift of writing. People who succeed need consistently healthy and unwavering support to continue to take daily strides and solidify positive movement toward their gifts. You are important, but remember you need family, friends, and coworkers as part of your support structure, as your personal cheerleaders alongside your own time commitment strategies.

When your resources are set up and you are already a few days into the process, it is time to really focus on your gift and chase it down. Push yourself out the door or wherever it is you must go to engage with your gift. Move to your drawing table and sit down. Go to a gym and hit the bike or weights. Join a welcoming running group. Go wherever you must go to set the stage for action. If you can stick to your resolve for at least six months or more while developing your new gift (42), you will have set enough of a pattern so that the gift is going to feel more familiar and you will feel more at ease tapping into your potential in this new aspect of your life. The most basic application of endurance is to launch into your gift and stick with it for enough time that you become hooked. You literally get to the point that—like my need to get out and run and write every day—you feel the desperate need to do the activity that reinforces your gift every day! Doing so adds further meaning and value to your day. I have been known to land after a 14-hour flight, get to my hotel, change into my gear, and hit the streets, even for a short tap into my running gift and even if my night is their day. Time has no bearing on my inspired action. The urgency you will feel will help you to endure while reminding you that you are committed to being all you can be. You are acting on your pledge to persist when others are resting and sleeping off whatever life demand depleted them this day. Once you are hooked, the world is yours to discover through your gift. You will be able to shape and refine your gift and eventually get to the point where you will be able to apply it in performance and transcend to a level of excellence you could only see in your mind's eye—a topic we discuss next in lesson six.

Overcoming Barriers to Excellence

Based on what I have learned from performers from many different disciplines, another important lesson must also enter the fray. Enduring is not a linear path, even when we start a new pursuit and anticipate a smooth ride to success. Your success story will experience setbacks along the way, ones you will need to find a way around or through (43). I have watched UFC athletes, kick boxers, martial artists, equestrians, figure skaters, shooters, ice hockey players, and athletes from a spectrum of sports disciplines who need to be physically and emotionally committed and dominant but instead become accepting, passive, and subservient when faced with a fierce hardship. These hardships may include personal injury, a powerful opponent, stiff competition, or an unaccepting coach. Visual telltale signs are evident in any person giving in to the will of an external force when earlier, they were happily chasing down their gifts. Pugilists, people in the combat sports, make their bodies appear smaller when they think they cannot overcome an obstacle, and to the eye, they attempt to protect themselves from the onslaught of blows they are receiving from their adversary. An international marathoner I worked with spoke of feeling physically smaller after the very first time in each race when she was inevitably elbowed out of the way by an opponent. She would then relent by moving aside and making way for her competitor to pass. Some athletes choose in their moments of hardship to reduce their commitment to their gift and retreat into a posture resembling a tortoise hiding in its shell. There is a feeling of being overwhelmed and of being conquered by hardship. Sometimes we avoid touching the experience of being stalled in a gift pursuit because of the emotional pain associated with disappointment, such as shame or guilt. It may be easier not to touch the hot potato of having let go of something you wanted so very much and just swallow the loss. At least for a time, the will to stand up for what the performer knows to be true about their gift—that is, what was built over days, months, and years of blood, sweat, and tears—no longer exists. Have you experienced being on this perfect path, smoothly moving toward one of your amazing gifts, when you suddenly faced an insurmountable barrier that elbowed you off course? Did you slow down or halt in your tracks as you went through this heavy adversity? What was your immediate emotional response? What was the longer-term consequence?

After a few passive performances, the athletes and those who work with them need to quickly find a way to help the performer recommit to enduring. The athlete needs to remember once more how to fight for what they want. Discussions must begin by making sense of previous performances when the athlete gave way to challenges that stopped them in their tracks instead of pushed them sufficiently to overcome and chase down their excellence. We then dig deeper into the chain of events before the athlete first softened in the will to endure (44). The athlete must come to understand the triggers and starting points that spark the chain of events that jeopardizes their will to endure, which ends in giving over their glimpses and the resulting investment in action to someone or something else. The trigger might be a tactical mistake, such as being caught out of playing position, resulting in being struck down by an opponent. If the sport is snowboarding or figure skating, the trigger could be the split-second beginning of a shift where physical balance was altered before it was lost. Tactical errors are commonplace for all people who dare to pursue their glimpses. You will be out of perfect position in your life many times over because you are human and, therefore, wonderfully imperfect. During moments of uncertainty, your default might be to concede or to be overtaken, resulting in passivity or shrinking back from acting with determination. Submission might not have been your initial default behavior when you first launched into building up your gift, but at some point it has become your default if you are no longer fighting for your gifts and your vision of enjoying them to the fullest. When you look more closely into the series of events that led up to you giving in, you will learn your decision to misstep was a conscious one—that is, a decision *not* to tap into your will and determination when it was needed most or a decision to respond with less effective battle strategies. Understanding you and the actions that have taken you off your path is a necessary step in any further development of your ability to endure and withstand subsequent challenges. Learning from little setbacks while you are shaping your gift will make you much stronger, and your ability to endure will be strengthened by improved self-awareness.

So, what have you learned from this second layer of enduring through a setback after following the developmental path of building up that gift? You must learn the takeaways and make sense of each of your missteps, either alone or with support from someone who can help guide you toward your gifts. Unpacking the setback is a necessary step if you want to channel your energy once more and return to your path. The process of understanding needs to happen quickly. Professional athletes who do not debrief, meaning they don't make sense of their setbacks, stall out quickly and recover slowly, if at all (45). Their metaphoric tires can no longer gain traction in soft dirt, a process needed for them to return to solid pavement where they can accelerate. Debriefing with some of the professional athletes I inherited sometimes occurred after several years of their not understanding a faltering performance. These athletes retained their promise, but on the precipice of once more performing at the highest level, they experienced a significant loss of confidence in their chances of winning (46). With their disbeliefs also came the lack of endurance to take them to the ring or starting line. Understanding not only what your setback was but why it happened and how to manage a similar setback next time is a necessary part of learning how to endure in a quest toward each gift. Within the same day you fall into a rut—such as when you lose your incentive or opt out of an opportunity to press your gift into action in some part of your life—recognize your choice for what it was and why it happened. You hit a road bump and went one direction when you should have chosen the other, sort of like drivers who instinctively steer away from instead of into a skid. The driver who steers away from the skid loses all control of the vehicle and ends up in a ditch.

Lean into your setback, pick yourself up, and examine the experience, ideally the very same day it happens. If you had a bad day at work because people did not respond to you when you were trying out some new communication strategy with colleagues in an important meeting, with your superior in attendance, look beyond where you stalled out to when exactly it happened. Did someone look at you in a funny way, which then made you wonder whether your enhanced approach should be abandoned? While you were thinking about the one isolated look instead of returning to your own body and mind, did you forget to refocus on what you were saying and all the people you were communicating with as opposed to one person? Did your loss of concentration cause a continued lack of focus throughout the day? Did the setback affect you in the workplace for the entire day or even beyond that day to other meetings when you could have spoken up? The lesson is that sometimes you will lose your focus and concentration when under pressure as you work on a gift. If you understand the chain of events that led to your setback and the pursuit of the gift, it becomes short term. You then return to your gift pursuit strengthened by a deeper insight about what is needed to succeed while managing some of your potential triggers. On a deeper level, you will also be rewarded by a confidence in your desire to endure. If you choose to endure in the gift you are pursuing, there is always a way through setbacks so you can continue your journey.

Understanding a misstep that diverts you from a gift pursuit is only the first step in your recovery and your return to progression. Next, you need some mind strengthening exercises, much like a body requires strengthening exercises before bearing heavy weight. One part of human endurance is well documented in scientific and practical writing, and it relates to learning how to develop and then use more constructive explanations when you stumble on your path (47). Previously externalized excuses, such as a common human tendency of blaming someone else when you should be taking ownership, known as a fundamental **attribution error** (48), should be replaced with a focus on your accountability and all actions under your direct control. Focus on better-directed effort and more emphasis on your personal gifts and abilities, both physical and mental. Within most workplaces, unhappy people are quick to assign the blame for their current dissatisfaction onto someone else. However, if you find yourself in a work or life situation where you have fallen into a similar pattern, dare to consider your role and influence and try to explain the circumstances more equitably, even when you run the risk of feeling short-term sadness or frustration with yourself. Question your role and responsibility in each misstep, no matter what, in relation to each stalling out experience. Only then can you return to working with the gifts you bring to your workplace. The same rule applies to your personal life and your hobbies. Although you can do some of this work on your own by strengthening your self-reflection, you can further reinforce your more constructive response through a healthy buddy system. Ask a trusted friend or family member who is able and committed to helping you develop your targeted gift to push you constructively each day, especially when you are working through a stumbling block. Your supporter should challenge your interpretations as opposed to being supportive of your sadness and frustration or remaining silent and standing by neutrally, neither of which is a healthy version of support. I often help athletes identify their debilitative words and develop useful counterarguments to evaluations where they are skirting responsibility through words that encourage apathy. If an athlete uses characteristics to describe themselves such as "I am weak" or "I am so stupid," they are replaced with more hopeful words like "I softened my will" or "I just didn't think." Otherwise, the person in hot pursuit of a gift can never dispute any inaccuracies, a practice termed ***disputing*** (49). Without a supportive and sometimes corrective force to help people regain their footing, they will become helpless because they believe their efforts do not match with those needed to return to success (50). My presence is a reminder, helping athletes return consistently to more useful explanations of any future challenge so they can sustain their engagement and chase down their glimpses for long enough that the chase becomes their pattern, and the pattern materializes into a full-blown gift.

Be prepared, because you might become frustrated with your designated supporter if this person does the necessary job. Accountability is a hard thing to be called out on. You might be okay with it at first and then become frustrated as the process continues. However, if you allow and encourage your friend to challenge you and reword your interpretations when you hit a road bump, the support will be invaluable. Evidence shows that an effective social support resource must sometimes challenge you; at times, it is the most important supportive action alongside praise (51). If you stick to the process of challenging yourself and allowing yourself to be challenged by your friend, you will be even more assured of getting at your gift. Choose your peer wisely and stick with the person and the process, never taking the feedback personally.

The boutique angle on how to strengthen your capacity to endure involves pushing forward from thinking and words to testing your endurance by adding strategic challenges to your daily life. There is a difference between theory and real-life situations. Life is relentless; people need to be confident in their skills and abilities to respond to daily challenges that trigger their negative thinking, apathy, or misdirected effort. One athlete client always struggled when performing against opponents who were either dirty in their game plan or brutally strong. The client did not like any form of confrontation. The athlete's default was to surrender superior skills and retreat into a passive style of performance that focused on survival. Every effort was directed toward self-protection, when the athlete simply needed to use superior skills within sports and in life outside of sports. The athlete's default response of defending and retreating was replaced with more effective strategies we developed by putting pen to paper. We worked hand in hand to identify triggering scenarios that posed challenges unique to this athlete's willingness to endure. After the scenarios were identified, the next step was to fully unpack each compromising situation and the athlete's typical response. Next, the athlete was tasked with designing sports scenarios in which the process included the ideal pathway through the challenge, with the athlete overcoming the previously insurmountable challenge. I also asked the athlete to consider scenarios that began well and then deteriorated, followed by effective pathways back to success. We then developed mental rehearsals oriented toward the style of play necessary to execute their skills. Scenarios were set up in which the athlete diverted from the ideal strategy and needed to scratch and claw all the way back into their winning performance. Mental rehearsal scenarios were then introduced in daily training and test **simulations**, slowly but surely, given the inevitable time line before us. The happy ending for this athlete was an expedited qualification to a world event, a profound tournament result, and a broader life lesson I hope will be integrated into daily living as a transferable skill.

You could follow a similar path of progression, where you build gradual confidence around your previously challenging situations whether they are exchanges with people or tough work or life circumstances. Think, speak, and physically design environments that test your resolve little by little. Your right pace is one that feels to you like a stretch but does not overly strain your confidence and ability to make effective decisions in the heat of the moment. Only then will you have a skill set to draw on when needed. Your task is to identify the physical contexts where you begin to feel or act in a weakened state. Perhaps your context is a workplace meeting where you need to pitch an idea, such as the earlier example, or maybe you are not great at thinking on your feet in a situation where you really want to be, such as when arguing your position in a workplace exchange of ideas. Take a good look at your typical actions and reactions and begin to consider your desired response. You might typically shut down and become silent, accepting another person's viewpoint even when you see a better alternative. Someone might argue for a jobsite practice, such as working behind closed office doors, but you feel a better flow of information happens when people share workspaces. The argument for a closed-door office might be the need to concentrate or it might simply be standard operating procedure. Your personal belief might be that people who think and work alone cannot arrive at the most creative solutions. You also do not believe that past practice means a rule should exist for the ages. Begin to prepare your viewpoint before ever sharing it. Begin by mapping out your ideas on a piece of paper or on your computer. At the top of the page, write the objective, meaning the position you want to propose. Next, develop a series of arguments in favor of your idea. If you are advocating a different approach for employees in the workplace, then explain your position based on some evidence why your approach has worked in similar work environments. Build your logic using simple points, with one point in the argument flowing logically into the next. Just by building your argument, you will begin to feel like the athlete building momentum and swaying the will of those in front of you toward the more collaborative workplace vision you see in your mind's eye. Next, look at your argument points and try to anticipate how these will be responded to. I identified the vintage counterargument of those not wishing for change, such as when people say, "Things have always been done this way" or "We are using best practices." What would be your counterargument to the resistance you anticipate?

Once you have your ideas set and you can see some of the potential resistance to your viewpoint, you will have the knowledge to develop a simulation strategy with responses for several scenarios. The responses you need to prepare for should include when everything goes just perfectly and people accept your idea, meaning your ideal situation, as well as a few situations in which things might be a bit sticky due to resistance, and you must manage resistance on the spot. Things can go either way, so be ready for both possibilities. In sport psychology, we sometimes refer to these general responses as mastery (52) and coping (53) scenarios, when things go as planned or not as planned, thus necessitating an alternate strategy. Begin with five deep breaths to center your thinking and your body. Your best delivery of your gifts flows from a mind and body that are clear and when your energy is concentrated on the task in front of you. Then, feel and see yourself from the perspective where you see your hands in front of you and the people nearby who you will be pitching to. Hear the discussion of ideas from others and listen carefully; when the time is right and you see an opening, take a deep breath and lay out your argument with strength and softness balanced. Notice how you feel confident, logical, and strong, with an open posture and a wonderful cadence in your voice. Continue to deliver your argument. Recognize the dissenting expressions and views and acknowledge them for their merits. Each view brings its own value. Slowly lay out how your ideas are an evolution for everyone in your workplace, building on detailed facts. Draw on all evidence you already have at your fingertips while tying in the views of others with different views as best you can. Conclude with a smile and an open expression. Once you have completed the mental rehearsal of your scenario, where your delivery was smooth and your gift well used, try it out in front of the mirror. During this process, if you feel you need a few brief notes, have these in your hand, and you can reference them as needed. Next, ask one or a few trusted friends to listen to your pitch and raise questions and other views. You should share with these trusted friends what some of the anticipated resistance might be so they can raise the concerns and you can then practice responding with composure and engagement. See how you, like the athlete, are building the readiness to deliver your gift step by step?

Reflecting on all that has been said in this lesson, your forward motion is going to require planning so you can draw on your glimpse and press it into action. Action is a necessary step when it comes to living out your gifts. The initial action will be exciting and rewarding as you unpack your gift. However, you also need the skills and motivational reminders to keep you on your path toward the gift. Some of these reminders will be ones you create and post to your walls. Others will be provided by the people who are your champions reinforcing your strengths. Once you are on the path and have all the supports in place, you will need to endure, meaning you will need to place one foot in front of the other even when you feel you are not progressing fast enough to your desired destination. Marathoners at certain points in their endurance events hit walls where they become exhausted and lose sight of their progress; yet they continue to progress. Road bumps, all of which are emotionally and sometimes physically painful, are inevitable parts of the journey to your desired destination. Challenges along any path are necessary and useful to you because they are meant to test resolve and commitment to your vision. Battles, such as a gift pursuit, need to be fought before they can be won. With the investment of time and energy, you will endure and your gift will become an integral part of who you are each day. In fact, a time will come when the gift you have just tapped into will be so important to you that you will carve time out every day to be fulfilled by drawing from it. You will crave its fulfillment.

⚠ Action Item Five: Enduring Through Your Words, Images, and Physical Actions

By this stage you have reengaged with your gifts; identified the people, activities, and organizations in your life that support your desire to fully realize your gifts; developed counters to the forces you experience in your life that may take you from your path; and have envisioned your future directions with the creation of a vision board or mandala. These action steps have helped you carve out your path, the path you must set to help achieve the best version of yourself. Now is the time to endure because your path will be long and winding and sometimes on pavement or in the dirt. Paths are rarely without twists, turns, potholes, bumps, and even unkind weather. Watch where you step while also leaning your body in the right direction, just as you lean into wind on a blustery day.

The action of enduring includes three interrelated pieces. First, work consistently and relentlessly on words, both inside your head and what you say to those in the world around you. Use a pocket journal and listen carefully to what you are thinking and saying. The words you choose must place you at the center of accountability for your actions. When you take accountability for an action, either a step or a misstep, take the time to write down what you said verbatim. When you draw on language that wears away at your desire to endure, meaning you either devalue your personal gifts or externalize the accountability of your misstep to someone else, take the time to write it down as well. No one is perfect in their tendency to take ownership at first. Sometimes you will forget to chase down your gifts, at least for a time. Recognize the words you use, and move in the direction of drawing upon the words that encourage your endurance and less on words that discourage forward movement and hope. Your effective choice of language is a skill set always in need of further practice; it is essential to your evolution. Be mindful of your words and draw on your self-affirmations to counter any negative thinking in moments of frustration.

You also need to imagine yourself enduring and being the most relentless version of who you are and what you stand for each day. Think of impending scenarios in which you really wish to persist and reinforce a specific asset or skill, such as arguing your point with conviction at a board meeting, a school council meeting, or a neighborhood forum on an important environmental issue. Be as precise as possible when building up your **imagery**, meaning the room or outside environment you identify. Add weather or room temperature, any people involved, time of day, and so forth—all of the nuances. Then, in either a seated or reclined position, visualize yourself walking into the situation so it becomes familiar. Play out the scenario in your mind, where you are asserting yourself with confidence, certainty, and enthusiasm from the beginning of the scenario through to a logical conclusion where you deliver your performance. Imagine yourself in a strong posture using clear and relevant words with the right balance of emotion, knowledge, logic, and belief. Notice how you are perfectly at home in the scenario, clear and positive minded, just being in the moment, attentive to and in harmony with the situation. If at any time you lose concentration and find you are engaging in an image where you are journeying toward uncertainty and a position of weakness, be patient, be resilient, and redirect yourself back into an assertive mindset. Images are like clay; they take time to mold into an artistic, exciting, beautiful form. The trick is to begin this process at least one week in advance of your important performance event to allow for the forming of your images through a daily application into their clearest, most resilient, and truest picture. Engaging in an exercise to reinforce endurance is a studying exercise, requiring time each day for you to become comfortable with the action in your mind's eye in advance of its delivery in real life. One word of caution: All exercises related to your endurance, physical or psychological, should be completed before early evening time so as not to stimulate your creativity and excitement when you should be relaxing and preparing for a full night's sleep and much-needed recovery.

Finally, you must put your endurance skills into action. Much like the high-performance athlete, your commitment to action is where your tire's rubber meets the road. Tackle scenarios that either intimidate, fluster, or challenge you, always beginning with easy scenarios. Rome was not built in a day; likewise, your ability to endure in any challenging situation, where you are to muster your best self, needs to be progressive in difficulty. I like to map out scenarios with increasing difficulty, starting with simple situations, in which an athlete's gifts can be reinvigorated and successfully put into action. Then begin to add challenges, such as throwing in a surprise situation in place of a planned one or inserting a slightly more difficult version of the original scenario. For example, if a runner is preparing for a race and committing to run it at a certain pace, the image might begin with the person running the standard alone; running with a few people; running in physically cramped scenarios where competitors push and touch one another, shoulder to shoulder; and finally, running in less-than-optimal weather conditions. See how the challenges are layered, one built on top of the previous? When the athletes encounter scenarios in which they find themselves strained and their resolve waivers, I work with the athlete and stop the physical rehearsal (a simulation). After a quick debrief, the athlete continues with new strategies to respond to the challenge at this current level before transitioning to the next stage of challenging situations, which will be a little more complex.

Another example illustrates the process. I once worked to prepare several large corporations in the service industry for the World Service Championships. The people I was working with were frontline workers in a high-profile fast-food company. We needed to work together so they could be the fastest and highest quality frontline workers in the competition. We soon realized that their speed on the production line was slowed by a lack of communication among coworkers who should have been working in concert. First, I watched them do their frontline work as they did it every day. Keep in mind these were the fastest of the frontline workers selected from a global food company. As they began to pick up speed and food was being fried up, there was a disconnect in the communication from those producing the food to those bringing it to the buyer. This disconnect was a source of frustration and a fracture in the team's ability to endure for the time needed to complete their competition event. The friction within the team rippled like electricity. We sat down already knowing where the team was stuck in the execution of their gift of fast service. In our discussion everyone agreed they had a shared vision of working seamlessly. The question they wanted addressed was how to coordinate the team's members for the smoothest and most efficient execution of their interdependent roles. First, we developed a series of four group affirmations, much like the ones you were introduced to. Next, we developed a group mental rehearsal script built from some of the most important skills they needed such as being in the present, continuous communication, and seeing themselves, much like a 4 × 100-meter relay team, where one fast athlete passed the baton to the next with smooth efficiency. We added in the emotional response of what it would feel like when things went smoothly, and they were literally flying through their work. Next, we explored some of the potential things that typically go wrong in the handoff process from one member to the next from the start of the task to its delivery in this cyclical process of production to delivery. Then we took what we knew and physically worked the process of production, slowly increasing speed, until an inefficiency resulted. We then debriefed, began again, a little slower than when we left off, until the team worked full steam at its best. Then the management and I introduced some deliberate distraction they knew was coming. The team needed to respond, recover, and return to top-class speed. Finally, we tried to surprise the team with potential missteps and had them work the problem, recover, and surge again. This fast-food example was one I presented long ago to colleagues in my field, all of whom found the work humorous. However, what I learned, just as you already know, is that the applications from elite and professional sports are transferable to all kinds of achievement settings where people are invested in the excellent delivery of their gifts.

So, what is the takeaway from this frontline service story? Harden your skills and don't merely endure ones already well practiced within comfortable scenarios in work, relationships, and play. The performer in you needs to be versatile and eventually able to manage a series of progressively challenging experiences when circumstances will prove challenging. The various scenarios you build into and the difficulties you identify will develop a gifted performer who is agile and ready to stand the test of a challenge when it inevitably arises in your world. The mental agility needed to respond under pressure is something most people tend to avoid because it is uncomfortable, but then again, it should be uncomfortable as you are stretching yourself. Growth is never comfortable because it is unfamiliar and therefore unsettling. On the other hand, your commitment when building your endurance is to tackle whichever test is put in front of you and approach it with conviction; conquer it through physical, emotional, and psychological stamina; and extend your ability to overcome all pressure. You will not be able to identify every possible complexity when you are building one of your gifts. However, when you can think through possible pitfalls through various levels of challenge, from the easy to the most difficult, the way you effectively manage yourself will be something you can count on when the time comes to really test your mettle.

⏰ Lesson Reminders

- ❖ You will be asked many times in life to endure as you reach for your gifts. Gifts are something every person holds, but not all people choose to endure in the pursuit of their gifts, nor do they have the know-how to endure. Desire without know-how is wishful thinking. Be fully engaged with your gifts and build the necessary skills to refine and add to your gifts over your lifetime.

- ❖ Work on skills that will help you stay on track as you move forward toward your gifts. Some of the skills are found in the previous lesson about glimpses, such as improved recognition of when they are happening and sufficient consideration of the opportunity being glimpsed. The skills provided in this lesson are about enduring and include the use of artifacts, self-affirmations, healthy support from the people around you, and progressive exposure to challenging situations, where you build confidence in your ability to endure.

- ❖ Endurance is a process that starts when you have identified and explored your glimpse and carries forward to its daily practice. Endure each day; the process of enduring toward a gift is at first exciting, and then potentially less exciting. The first few days will bring a glitter to an exciting application of a gift, but you should work with your gift for a minimum of 6 months before it really begins to take hold as an important and deeply desired part of your day. Especially for the first 6 to 12 months, stick it out and draw on every resource of energy suggested in this book, as well as further ideas you can create and build positive energy from to reinforce your gift. If you endure, your glimpse and resolution to act will lead to an even more vibrant version of your giftedness that is solidly formed.

- ❖ Enduring is a challenge faced by every aspiring performer—athlete, coach, employee, educator, or author. Somewhere along the way you might have lost momentum in the pursuit of one of your gifts and never circled back to it. The potential loss you experienced was left untouched for a time. If there is a part of your past when a valued gift was set aside, enter the debriefing process I provided in this lesson, identify the root parts of where things went wrong, and grab the lessons you have learned about your response, such as when you stopped, why you stopped, and how you were accountable in the decision to stop. Next, learn from the debriefing process and apply it to your endurance of a gift pursuit. Either tap into your previous gift as it was once enjoyed, or from this point forward, debrief when you are slowed in your progression of a new gift due to a setback so that you can speed up recovery and further your endurance.

THE MENTAL PERFORMANCE CONSULTANT

Over the years, the developing professor, now an established mental performance consultant to international-level athletes, has attended many major sporting events and lived among these athletes in the final days leading up to their performance opportunities. The major games village where they reside is a small city, with newly built residences and amenities. The athletes move into the village four or five days before the major games event. The relocation into this new living space is a jolting experience. The athletes and staff gain their accreditation, walk through security, get their nation's clothing package, and then they walk among their teammates to their dormitories to drop off their clothing and equipment and explore their new environment. The sheer excitement of walking among performers from every part of the world is spellbinding, with each country's colors on display through flags and sport uniforms. There is a celebratory feeling within the confines of the village. The feeling of excitement continues for three or four days as the athletes get into the groove of final training culminating in that moment, where they are to meet and exceed past performances. They are seeking to transcend, and to do so, those who are supporting them, including the mental performance consultant, must do the same and become even more efficient and ingenious with their skills.

The former protégé, now a mentor, knows well from days past how excitement wanes and the realities and expectations will begin to weigh on their minds. Team discussions and his individual work with the athletes reinforce the application of daily living routines within an unusual environment, normalizing it as healthy and ripe with possibilities. The hardest request of the athletes is asking them to be themselves in temperament, perspective, and values within an environment full of distractions and modeling versions of self that are inauthentic and not in their best interest. The mental performance consultant meets with each athlete and the group each day. He is often seen taking walks and sitting on park benches with athletes in the farthest reaches of the secure village. Quietness in a very exciting living environment needs to be found so that he and the athletes can have genuine, honest, deep conversations, during which the athletes can be truthful with themselves and the mental performance consultant about how they are feeling and what they anticipate as the possibilities and barriers to their excellence. They need to express and normalize concerns about the delivery of their gifts on a highly visible stage. The athletes need to come face-to-face with their fears and anxieties and let these feelings out as opposed to internalizing them. The athletes need to be simmering in the right mindset before they can perform, with their energies contained and at the ready. Each athlete is monitored with care as the event draws closer. They make the gradual transition from being excited to being task focused. They recognize each day must be used to help them progress in the final steps before they can transcend previous performances. In the final 24 hours before their first event, the athletes turn their focus to a brief performance review, relaxation, meditation, a good night's rest, and then a readiness to launch into their extraordinary version of performance. During these final hours, in conversations with the mental performance consultant, he slips in a very important reminder to each athlete. Theirs is a path less traveled by people living without transcendence as a coveted experience. He reminds each of the athletes to remember the people they pass each day going about their business in regular, perhaps monotonous jobs. The athletes need to recognize and embrace their gifts and how fortunate they are to live these gifts out at the highest level. The pending performance is an opportunity to be seized and savored. With the full recognition of the opportunity before them, the athletes need to suspend their fears and embrace their uncertainty beyond which possibilities abound.

For the athletes, the village signifies the realization they are about to step onto a world stage and revel in their moment. They hold the potential to deliver their version of the extraordinary in front of a live audience, where they can test themselves against the best of the best. Similarly, you will experience lead-up days in advance of performances monumental in your life where you can perform your gifts at the highest level. The village is a metaphor for the physical and mental home ground you must live in and acclimate to before launching into your next exceptional performance. The village might include a hotel and workplace environment that are new to you, such as when you seek out an exciting new position. Alternately, you might be in a situation much like a professional athlete who at times performs on home ground. Although you are living in your home in the days leading up to your performance, your focus must slowly narrow to your epic performance, such as pitching a new business idea to a financial lender, your employer, or your employees. When you prepare for the performance event, you must acclimate to the pending pressure. Amid this final leg in the lead-up to your performance, you must act as you normally would, with a healthy perspective, living each day as it comes. You must go for walks, enjoy your meals, and instill normality instead of becoming distracted by the inevitable glimmer of the pending performance or overwhelmed by last-minute cramming of what you should already know and the uncertainty that accompanies these unwise actions. Either call upon a wise sage in your life (your version of the mental performance consultant) to touch base with during your final lead-up to the performance, or imagine you have a wise sage sitting on your shoulder helping you navigate the final few crossroads before you launch into performance and helping you make true and healthy decisions in advance of your transcendence. If your touchstone is the wise sage on your shoulder, symbolizing your best judgment, always default to the concept of trusting yourself and doing only necessary tasks as opposed to filling your day with busywork. I have cautioned many performers against leaving their best selves in the final moments of preparation by doing too much or not valuing sound decisions, which can come at the expense of transcending and the inevitable result—gifting yourself.

LESSON SIX
TRANSCENDENCE

> *The soul should always stand ajar, ready to welcome the ecstatic experience.*
>
> Emily Dickinson

When you retrace your steps from life's detours and systematically strengthen your skills, you can endure on your chosen path, as you have to this point in the book. The next step in your journey is to reach a stage at which your abilities, efforts, and commitment are pulled together and you fully perform your gifts in the moments you have dreamed about, even overdelivering and performing beyond your expectations. The performer in you undergoing transcendence will feel much like land at sunrise, where your geography, previously darkened and untested, will become vibrant through the sun's light and ready to use. Although you can prepare systematically to use your gifts, you can also win and lose in their delivery when success is just within your reach.

One of the most memorable segments of the movie *Ali* is well known to lovers of prize fighting, given the odds against Muhammad Ali's winning. George Foreman was known to be a one-man wrecking crew who decimated every opponent he faced as an amateur Olympic champion and then as a professional boxer. Ali was certainly headed to an inevitable and painful loss in a blockbuster world championship fight scheduled to happen in Kinshasa, Zaire, known as the "Rumble in the Jungle" (54). However, something remarkable happened that was captured meaningfully by the film—the prevailing of the human spirit. While the two boxers were acclimating to the oppressive African heat during the country's hot season, the bout was postponed because Foreman's right eye was cut while he was sparring. For the eight days of delay that followed the injury, Ali connected with the local community. He ran with them, talked with the children, spent time among the people, and ultimately became an adopted son of the community. He also used those extra eight days to gather his internal resources and strengthen his resolve for the fight that lay ahead. He was surrounded by people who visibly were touched by his plight of being the physically smaller, underdog opponent. On fight night, we see Ali lead a somewhat somber entourage into believing in his ability to overcome a much bigger and more powerful opponent. He claims to have found the answer to the riddle of how to transcend on that night, although he keeps his winning strategy to himself. Transcendence is something only he, the performer, can enact. In the opening round of the fight, Foreman starts strong, putting all his power into his punches because he anticipates a quick, punishing fight. All the while, Ali carefully picks his responses, and when the two boxers are in close quarters, Ali places all his weight on Foreman, quietly whispering in his ear. Over time, Foreman's extraordinary strength becomes less so as his energy reserves and determination deplete in the warm night. He has been brought strategically by Ali to a state of physical exhaustion that he could not have imagined. During the next few rounds, we watch Ali sitting on the ropes, biding his time and waiting for the rest of Foreman's energy stores to hit bottom, while continuing to return punches strategically, slowly wearing down his opponent. A boxer may punch themselves out by showing too much of their physical and psychological game too soon and investing their reserves prematurely. Finally, the time comes when Foreman is completely exhausted and doubled over, almost unresponsive, and the smaller man, Ali, becomes the physically larger, faster, and more aggressive of the two. The hunted becomes the hunter. On that night, Ali beat extreme odds and transcended to a level of greatness unimaginable to anyone other than himself as he stopped Foreman in his tracks, dropping him to the canvas for the first time in a brilliant career.

The lesson from monumental sporting events like the one just described is that all the physical ability in the world means nothing unless you are savvy with your performance tactics under pressure, in the heat of battle. This lesson about transcendence is focused on what you should do as the time draws near so that you can deliver your performances of a lifetime when you choose to, especially when the odds are stacked against you. It's time to do those final few tactics and deliver your equivalent of a knockout punch and deliver your gift. This lesson will provide you with a useful road map, or performance plan, of how to organize the final days, hours, and minutes before your monumental performance to your best advantage (55). Then the lesson continues with suggestions on how to tap into your gifts during your performance so that you, like any exceptional athlete who delivers excellence, will transcend.

Defining Transcendence

Coaches and staff describe the transcendent athlete as someone who is shiny, glowing, radiant, and comfortable in their skin just before and then when they are under the bright lights. These are the people who are doing exactly what they should be doing, as they should be doing it, when the time is right. One of the oldest sayings shared with many a pugilist in the moments leading up to an epic battle by their staff is, "It is your time to shine." Sitting with athletes in their dressing rooms, the roar of the crowd audible outside the cinder block walls and passageways into their sport arenas, I have observed they are aware of their readiness in this, the final mile of their current performance. Athletes must shake off their inevitable final nerves, gather their internal resources into a beam of focus, and steel themselves for the epic battle before them—one they must fight for with conviction and endurance. There are times to shine in every person's life, but not all performers, even the best prepared, take their final step into the performance arena and commit when the moment of opportunity is within arm's reach (56). As a former national team athlete, I understand the difference between having a brass ring within reach and mobilizing the required inner resources to turn promise and possibility into action, reality, and then into part of one's life history. I experienced transcendence in large international sport competitions, but I also experienced performances that were not transcendent. My path toward and away from transcendence taught me all I needed to know to arm me for my current life, whether in my job, running events, family life, writing, scientific contributions, or anything else I attempted. As one personal example, the university path was one I always wanted and pushed toward with conviction, from childhood through graduate studies and onward. Upon reflection, I naturally went about my journey of closing one door as an amateur elite athlete and vigorously opening another based on a long-standing vision and the creative abilities I am gifted with. My choices required a hardening process, a withstanding of external forces, time, hard work, and an unbending knowledge of my potential, especially when others did not see, understand, or support my vision and the career transition that followed. I emerged as a scientist, educator, and practitioner. Then I transcended to the forefront of my domain as a world leader in the sport psychology society who now supports young aspirants from sport and my profession in their pursuit of transcendence.

To transcend requires you to move beyond your lingering doubts, fears, environmental barriers (naysayers), and any previous performance slumps or professional or personal contortions you experienced, and then to exceed the exacting standards needed to be the very best version of who you are meant to be when the time comes for you to tap into a gift and deliver it at your highest current level. Your task is to approach each moment of self-questioning as the days and hours wind down, knowing it will soon be your time to stand up, increase your presence, and live out your performance to your full and well-deserved scope, so you can ascend to the top and claim to your prize. The performance will culminate at first in that initial win. Once you transcend, recognize that you can tap into who you are and deliver your version of giftedness in whichever environment you choose, whenever you wish, for as long as your mind and body can withstand. The application of your transcendence to further opportunities will be discussed as part of lesson seven. Transcendence then is meant to become a transferable opportunity for you to carry in your body and mind from a work environment to a second work environment or to a personal scenario over the course of a well-lived existence.

One professional athlete I worked with for several years provides an example of transcendence. This boxer was on the precipice of greatness, already having achieved a world champion status. The gauntlet thrown down before him was to accept a challenge from one of the top adversaries in the sport and place a personal accomplished status on the line. Although he was a champion and opponents were of a very good quality, there was not yet an encounter with an opponent known to be vastly better than my client. Some pundits suggested he was untested at the highest level of the sport and that the test would be well outside his reach. In the months and weeks leading up to the globally televised fight, many naysayers anticipated an inevitable fall from grace, just as Ali was anticipated to fall from grace at Foreman's hands. The media and the opponent anticipated an exposure of the boxer as a paper champion and not one of true substance. The support team surrounding him understood what was at stake. This attempt at transcendence was risky but rich in opportunity to expand worldwide into rarefied thin air at the apex of a sport. If there was ever a moment where resolve was being tested, this boxer was undergoing the experience and its risk-to-loss ratio in full.

Together, the team affirmed what the boxer knew intuitively to be a wonderful opportunity to transcend a paper title and ascend to the apex of the sport's highest level. The question was: How can we put together a plan, piece by piece, to overcome the opponent before the performer and entourage? The opponent was profiled based on strengths, limitations, and behavioral patterns. For example, the opponent was a cautious person who took a long time to warm into performance. The boxer needed a sizable lead before the opposition was able to adjust style and strategy in the battle. The opponent's gaps fueled the boxer's knowledge and spurred the ability to adapt to a higher level of play than outsiders anticipated. We then formulated a winning strategy that would help the boxer meet the lofty objective posed by the opponent's renowned quality. We followed a format resembling the one I have already proposed to you in the previous lesson, where bricks and mortar—that is, affirmations and artifacts—were first put into place. The plan became clearer as we went along, and it was built around our client's performance style, including speeches to the press and tactics through the media leading up to the fight to affirm our client and destabilize the opponent. Finally, we formulated a special battle plan in the days, hours, and minutes leading up to the big moment. My job was to stay with the client in the days before the fight and ensure proper rest, psychological recovery, positive language in relation to the fight, and reminders of the long journey that brought him to the current time where transcendence was near. During this process, he was fully engaged in the possibilities, never doubting or questioning the potential win. Then, in the final hours, sitting in the dressing room before the inevitable performance, the team members were certain we could hear the boxer's heartbeat in the dressing room, though likely, what we heard was our own heartbeats. Our hearts beat in sync; we stood united throughout the strenuous preparation and leap of faith. Our team had momentum, and much like the audience in Kinshasa, Zaire, the home audience sensed we were about to pull a rabbit from the hat in a display of sport magic.

The moment then arrived. The television crew stepped into the room and the camera and lights were upon the boxer and team, so close and so bright they emitted heat. Lights warmed the room, lights that would follow the performer from that moment until the end of the performance. Music and pyrotechnics boomed as we began to walk through the corridors and into the darkened arena that was filled to the ceiling with screaming fans and naysayers, all awaiting the spectacle to come. Some boxers would have decreased in size during that very moment, but this boxer grew larger in stature and poise. Forever a people watcher, I recognized the boxer responding with assurance, brimming with confidence as the performer's body slipped between the ropes and into the ring, radiating with belief. The performer was ready to perform. The opponent who stood waiting turned to look, and I recognized a telltale emotional expression—surprise and uncertainty. The opponent's face showed a sudden nagging question: Would he endure and succeed, or would this be the inevitable moment when he would relent under high pressure despite the anticipated great odds to win? In such moments, bodies and minds do more or less than they could, depending on the approach or avoidance response to the opportunity that awaits. These moments are tenuous and require a fortified version of the human performer where endurance materializes into reality and recognition.

Our lives are filled with challenging tests time and again. We step into the lights as either our partial or whole person. The fight just presented was a series of actions, and within minutes the opponent began a sharp descent from greatness to ordinary. Like Foreman, the opponent became someone unknown; this other questioning and contorted person in the ring was materializing in front of the boxing world as someone passive and accepting of someone else's will. Internal forces were to prevail for one boxer, and external counterforces were to rule over the other. All that remained was a shell of the highly touted boxer, to the point where they became ordinary, mechanical, slow, and reactive. The careers of these two boxers after that memorable night proved telling. The opponent who lost his way internalized only one lesson: to accept personal contortions in a path away from giftedness and toward being a passive follower. Much like the athletes and performers I discussed in lesson five, the opponent likely did not engage in a much-needed debriefing process. Sadly, he stepped off his true path without question or challenge, his amazing gift of athleticism was no longer used and it was lost for what remained of his career. The winning athlete, in sharp contrast to the defeated boxer, progressed with an illustrious career and many more accolades. My client would go on to win some of the most memorable sporting events, followed by losses, reinvention, and further successes. The lesson from this true story is that both athletes learned their own life lessons. They each mirrored what we have discussed throughout this book in terms of knowing one's gifts, struggling with competing forces, contorting, or staying true to oneself, glimpsing into a future, enduring, and flirting with transcendence. One athlete learned the boundless opportunities that exist when you endure and are systematic in your pursuits, whereas the other chose not to reflect and to accept a misstep without later correction. The consequence was a tormented performer who continued to decline and retired unfulfilled.

Guiding Principles for Transcendence

So, what do you need to know for you to transcend, an action that comes from just letting your performance flow out of you (57)? A guiding principle is to identify any concerns or question marks that are lingering while the event is still in the future, ideally, long before the final few days, if possible. Like most people, you will have nagging questions before each opportunity to perform as the fullest version of yourself. Monumental challenges, where you must put yourself on the line and expose your strengths and current limitations, take courage because they also reveal your vulnerabilities. Your courage and willingness to attempt transcendence is something you must test and attempt regularly to stretch your limits and your appreciation of them. The closer you get to each opportunity to shine, the more you will be tested on whether you will remain persistent in your pursuit and push your body and mind forward to action. Just as the best performers in the world face profound times of self-questioning as events loom closer to the moment when they must deliver, so too must you face your questions each time you seek to transcend.

In the lead-up to any opportunity to transcend, challenge each question mark that will come to the forefront of your mind by arguing with conviction for yourself and referring to past experiences that remind you that you are up for the task ahead. This skill of self-arguing is one we discussed in lesson five on endurance. I suggested that you should dispute any destructive thoughts that reinforce less effort and argue back with thoughts that you can succeed and remind yourself how you did it previously (58). Perhaps you are within two days of a sports competition, like a golf event, for which you have prepared several months. Within the final few days, you might begin to question your golf swing or more generally whether you are going to make a fool of yourself. You know there is still competition coming to the tournament. Only through standing up for your best application of your gifts in the face of self-questions or naysayers can you reduce or remove the last-minute question regarding whether you will be able to deliver your version of excellence when the time comes to let go and perform. So, face whichever question mark is in front of you when it arises and challenge it right back so that it doesn't loom large and take on a life of its own. When you are ready to take those final steps toward transcending, remember that it's normal for your mind to get the best of you and look to protect what you already have achieved in terms of results and reputation, where there is little to no risk of revealing any weakness. When it comes to your gifts, protecting past success because you believe you are also protecting your reputation is a form of self-sabotage. Protecting history limits your ability to reach for improvement and your next level of giftedness. Questioning is inevitable, but effective responses that push doubt back into healthy proportion is not always a given. Your job is to shrink self-doubt until it dissolves into a manageable size or nonexistence, clearing your path toward the gift you are pursuing.

A second founding principle is to always go with who you are (your true self) and the skills you have at hand based on systematic preparation. I have worked with professional ice hockey players seeking to enter the National Hockey League (NHL). These athletes often hold experience at Junior World Championships and have thrived in the feeder system, but they have not made it to the NHL. They already have their gifts; it is just a matter of applying them when surrounded by equivalent players who are already performing in the desired top league. Their gifts exist but they must be tested in a higher-level performance environment. Sometimes, in the final 24 hours before they get their chance to play in an exhibition game or are called up to replace an injured athlete, we will be on the phone a few times. The player will sometimes call from the hallway of a hotel so as not to disturb a roommate or because of fear of revealing their uncertainty to a potential teammate. The goal through our discussions is for the athlete to recognize their gifts are intact and ready. Each athlete must also shift their outlook from one of fear of failure to excitement of the possibility ahead, one that has been dreamed of for many years and from a very young age. People in these final few days and hours often want to overprepare. If they overthink or overtrain, their thinking and style of play can become robotic or they may become emotionally flat. These people remind me of the sorts of students who tend to be last-minute studiers for course exams and entry exams to medical and law school. You know the behavior I am speaking about—people who are trying to cram in those last bits of information before they walk into the exam hall and need to remember them. The best version of you is one prepared and seasoned over time, not one desperately packaged or revisited at the last minute before you attempt to transcend. Yet time and again, I see athletes seeking to put in that last workout, not permitting their minds and bodies to rest and fully recharged for the opportunity ahead. The result is always the same: It is damaging in terms of personal exhaustion, insecurity, and loss of feel for the gift. Instead of continuing to close the gap of time effectively, they widen the gap from their gift to its potential delivery. Hardly ever is last-minute preparation useful when it comes to delivering a transcending performance, where your shininess is needed. The days, hours, and minutes are meant to be times of quietness and trust in your systematic preparation, leading to clarity, readiness, and excitement for the opportunity ahead. At the same time, you are storing your resources and ensuring you are fully fueled and energized and ready to thrive. The only exception to the rule is if a little bit of playing with your gift is fun and only when it is briefly touched as a quick reminder. Ice hockey players may have an afternoon short practice, or boxers may practice a few moves the afternoon of their fight in a parking lot or hotel basement.

The days leading up to your opportunity to transcend should be filled with self-care and activities that counterbalance any depleting of resources caused by the anticipation you are feeling. The term *self-care* is one I often circle back to in applied work and even with students and young researchers. People seeking excellence focus far too much on performance expectations or a broader performance pathway and forget to balance out their days to permit for healing and physical and emotional recovery. Especially when you are on the precipice of excellence, your approach needs to be well rounded to foster well-being (59). Take care of yourself—sleep well, eat well, and maintain crucial social connections that help you with your perspective. Schedule in special treats, such as an afternoon coffee or tea, a movie, or other activities to balance out your time, such as a quiet walk with your dog. You cannot stay at a fever pitch 24 hours a day, especially not as an important life opportunity is fast approaching. Eat well on a proper schedule. Hydrate, just as an athlete would. Finally, relax in the evenings for several hours before falling to sleep. Time unplugged from social media, emails, and work needs to become a necessity from dinner time onward as your coveted performance opportunity is near. Just as you will need to be sharp and crisp to perform, there will be times in the final few days beforehand when you need to unwind and recharge for the battle ahead.

The third principle to transcending is your commitment to step up and be who you are meant to be under the bright lights and in the heat of pressure. The delivery of each transcendent performance you attempt needs to be authoritative from the start, just as racehorses break from the starting gate, committed boxers launch into their bouts from first bell, and concert musicians and their accompanying bands open their show with strong songs and a compelling beat. Immediately establish your rhythm and begin to deliver your gift in the way that you have prepared for and committed to during mental skills and simulations. Follow your logical plan—one that builds slowly but surely to its peak and is strategically designed to pull out your gifts. Sometimes the delivery of your plan goes exactly as you saw it in your mind's eye and unfolds as your best-case scenario. Sometimes you may be really battling hard with exertion, and at other times, your attempt to transcend is touch and go. These three general categories of possibilities—the best, worst, and most likely scenarios—are found in any strategy that includes the resilience exercise of decatastrophizing (60). When you prepare as an agile performer for several possibilities and ways to take charge of each one, little will phase you before and during your opportunities to thrive compared with people with a one-dimensional plan. In running events, when I am switched on and performance is flowing out of me, I am fully absorbed in the moment, going with the sensation—loving it. When I am in top flight, I can sense the front runners gasp deeper for air as their mouths open a little wider, searching for oxygen no longer accessible to them. In these moments, I know it is time to surge, and I do just that as I listen to my rhythm, foot strike blending into foot strike. I stick to my plan, monitor my mind and body, and make certain I have set a pace with just enough energy to cross the finish line, making the closing mile my most compelling. At other times I have struggled through stomach cramps and stitches in my side, such that I needed to slow my pace and watch my opponents gain ground as I temporarily lost reach. The most common reality for me is that the final few kilometers or miles of a race will be temporarily painful. You will feel unavoidable strain as you near the climax of your performance, having done everything according to your plan. You are stretching yourself thin at the right moment, when reserves should be at the point of nearing empty. With the finish line and final few minutes to seconds winding down, you must look inward, delay your recognition of feeling stretched thin, and commit to your rhythm. Then you must surge one last time, knowing that tiredness is the price you are paying to push beyond previous boundaries.

What you are doing in these small slivers of time is shattering your glass ceiling and enjoying the sensation that you are relentless, unlike others. Your pain is temporary, and your transcendent experience is permanently secured as part of your life history and potential success pattern. Victories in sport, business, and life are often hard fought and painful before they are won and surmounted. Each performance requires your unrelenting desire, strategic execution, stamina, grit, and a compelling commitment that carries you through to its logical and systematically executed end.

Achieving and Reflecting on Transcendence

Transcending is the result of a healthy process where you challenge yourself systematically over time on your pathway to a desired state of being. You have a good understanding of where you want to go and a process you have followed that was engineered from previous discussion topics. Any person who is well prepared, methodical, well rested, and self-assured holds the potential to exceed earlier levels of performance and move forward to the next level (61). What should you remember when preparing to take your final step and reaching inward to transcend? Recognize the process ending in transcendence is not for people looking to maintain their status quo, nor is it easily available for disorganized performers. The alternative to stepping up and committing to a transcendent performance as your true path is whatever opposes you being anything less than your potential. Then, make peace with the fact that the path before you will be a strain—it will likely be exhausting, it could be fearful—and you will most certainly have to fight for what and whoever you believe yourself to be. Before a road race, I know the pain to come, and frankly, it always troubles me before I steel myself and take off. Professional boxers and UFC fighters also know that they will take blows from their opponents and flirt with physical exhaustion. People around you will tend to pull back and slow down, not wanting to touch the depths of their endurance or pay the physical price in competition situations, but you must push yourself strategically out of your comfort zone as you seek to perform in each opportunity. Once you cross your type of finish line and your excellent performance is in the books, you will likely experience the same realization every Olympic medalist or professional champion has been known to identify in research (62): You will be astonished that all your lessons have been methodically performed and your anticipated win came so naturally to you. The time in preparation and wait has come and gone in the blink of an eye. You will also be surprised with how quickly you recover and how soon you wish for the next opportunity to further sculpt who you are or explore the next life challenge. No matter how bruised and battered a body or mind might be after delivering excellence, both heal rapidly. Mind and body then crave the next opportunity to push boundaries and to feel alive. As you seek to deliver excellence, you will want what a friend of mine refers to as "the thin edge of the wedge," in other words, a performance that is razor sharp.

The reflections on transcending are two. First, transcending needs to happen many times on your life path, and each opportunity should materialize into a progression toward your well-lived existence. Without stretching your boundaries, you will never be satisfied nor convinced you are living an extraordinary life. Why? Because you won't be. Second, people too often can transcend in one part of their life but forget that the lessons they learned in one situation are applicable to many other parts of their life. Once a performer, you have the potential to always be a performer. Yet many former world-class athletes appear lost after their athletic careers have come to an inevitable end (63). Some athletes look content several years after retirement, although far too many are sad and despondent as they reflect on a great past in place of a great present and an equally promising future (64). I was close friends with an Olympic wrestler who well into middle age continued to live out personal moments from an Olympics 30 years earlier instead of looking for new excellence opportunities and the discovery of new gifts. Some of the extreme cases of athletes lost to time fall on personal crisis because they cannot parlay well-learned processes that led to outcomes such as Olympic gold medals and world championship titles onto future possibilities (65). Examples from professional sports can be taken from boxing, ice hockey, the UFC, and Formula One. Thankfully, elite athletes in many sport systems are now being deliberately taught to plan for their postathletic careers long before this one exciting gift is no longer the resource it once was (66). Many sports performers feel lost when their professional careers end. What these same people forget are the tremendous transferable life lessons they gained, such as how to pursue a goal, train relentlessly, focus under pressure, recover systematically from a life test, work with teammates, and push forward after a setback. There are limitless places where you can apply your lessons of how to transcend, following processes you know work well for you as a person that you initially learned in one performance environment. These multiple opportunities to become even better at who you are in the broadest sense become wins, a topic we discuss next in lesson seven on symmetry. Just as you are your authentic self in one environment, delivering your version of excellence, you are the very same person wherever you go, no matter the environment. All you need to do is recognize the transferability of your uniqueness, apply your most effective pathway to delivering excellence, and live out to the highest level the new life opportunities you have glimpsed on your horizon. Growth and opportunity to transcend are always right around the corner. Seek out your next quest; prepare your plan, resources, and time line; and then take relentless action.

Action Item Six: Identify and Resolve Your Questions and Work Your Plan

In your quest for transcendence, you have followed a healthy process and worked on each action item already provided. The groundwork is always necessary to set the stage for any transcendent performance. In lesson five, you worked on progressive scenarios intended to strengthen and fortify your commitment and vision. Now is the time to take the foundation you have built, practiced, and tested in progressive circumstances and apply it into a performance opportunity you are coveting, such as a job interview, a sales pitch, a board examination or certification, an athletic competition, or something that is equally meaningful to you. Before you launch into the excellence of performance, nullify or reduce any lingering question marks or barriers to unleashing your gifts. There will always be question marks before any attempt to transcend; your job is to recognize them and then reduce them to a size where they can be overcome—where you can overcome!

Early in the final week before your important event, make a list of things that are lingering in the back of your mind as unresolved questions. The runner might wonder whether enough mileage, hill work, or speed were invested in their preparation. The person attempting a board certification or entry exam might wonder whether they know all their material before they come face-to-face with a panel of judges. A lawyer might wonder whether they have all the facts before pitching their argument to judge or jury. The person preparing for that important job interview might question whether they have enough and sufficiently deep information about the organization they are hoping to become part of. Many of these question marks can be reduced systematically. The questions need to be identified and acknowledged first and foremost. You must lay out these questions as early as possible in advance of the performance. Some may be easily addressed, such as the need for more rest, slight refinements in your battle plan, a sharing of the plan with the people who support you, and the gathering of important articles of equipment, such as clothing and accessories. As you list any of the logistic or content-related questions, set a time line of when each needs to be resolved. With the removal of each question mark, you will continue to feel and recognize forward momentum toward your performance. Some question marks on your list will remain with you all the way into the performance arena onward to when you engage in the performance. Identify each question mark you cannot dispel and examine it in its right perspective. Many of the unresolved questions are often much smaller when you look at them in relation to the hard work invested in your path to transcendence. Then, with the questions that cannot be fully resolved before you enter the performance, develop a list of the strengths you will use to counterbalance your existing questions. If you feel you have not had the perfect training plan for a sports performance, but that a lot of what you wished for was integrated, consider also how your ability to perform under pressure and some of your psychological and physical strengths will help you in your quest. The balance sheet will reveal that your gifts and readiness far outweigh the uncertainties you are feeling. Recognizing your balance sheet will put the probability of success where it belongs, leaning toward likelihood. At the same time, this sort of exercise will help save you from last-minute studying when you should be charging your battery and preparing to thrive.

Look to the different areas of your life, past and present, where you have applied a great, on-point strategy for the days of your human tests, the ones where you exceeded your previous versions of excellence. The experiences at the top of your game might include taking an important exam, previous successful job interviews, historic athletic performances, and any further transcendent experience where you aced the performance and moved beyond an earlier level of excellence. As you reflect on your previous experiences applying excellence, develop a list of the most outstanding of your performances, with one relatively recent experience that reflects your best version of who you presently are. In the days before you transcend, your belief needs to strengthen and not stay the same or reduce in size (67). From what we know about building self-confidence, how you apply your best version of yourself will always be transferable from one part of your life to another. People make a sizable mistake when they disregard their life experiences and present their current opportunity to transcend as something vastly different from anything previously experienced. Opportunities to transcend will be available in many parts of your life, and yet your pattern to transcend, meaning your method to reach this state, will be quite similar across diverse parts of your life. Recognize the transferability of your gift and draw strength from as many parts of your life as you can. If you are a great test taker, you are a great performer under pressure, period.

Next, look at your final 24-hour structure before the opportunity to transcend, step by step from the time you intend to sleep, the number of hours in sleep, how you feel when you wake up, onward to the activities structured into the day as it narrows to the final hours and final minutes, the walk into the performance area, and then to the performance. What sorts of activities have you planned? Do these make sense in terms of being rested, with an increasingly narrow focus for when the time comes to deliver the performance? What sorts of food and drink will work best and when should you take them to balance basic physiological needs with nerves? As you review your plan and consider these questions, remember that the day of performance is one where you must go with the skills you've already developed and with your version of a plan as opposed to anyone else's. As I say to athletes, "Go with what you've got." Although the statement sounds like a cliché, when you have done all the groundwork in advance of the performance, there must come a time where you trust in the work and stand by its quality, much as you would stand by a personal value, such as being honest and courageous. Trust in your work and settle into your methodical approach in place of trying to do last-minute touch-ups on your battle plan in those final hours before you launch into action. Granted, a methodical approach that permits time to compose and reflect might be counterintuitive as opposed to filling your day with needless work, but do it anyway. Stick to your preset plan with conviction and execute it with a clear mind and full commitment. The dust must settle before you wage battle so that you can see the horizon before you. Even for the best-prepared athletes, battles are often won and lost in the final day before the performance due to wise or unwise expenditure of focus and energy, where logic and self-confidence sometimes wage war with the counterforce of uncertainty and insecurity (68).

Every wise performer needs to develop two plans: one in which you are prepared for things going exactly according to plan; and one in which things happen, the plan goes astray, and you need to circle back to your plan. One Olympian was so surprised in his first encounter with a world champion in his sport by how easy his performance came. The athlete was in the middle of pulling off a surprise upset when he self-sabotaged. Many performers are not prepared for their ideal circumstance, yet the ideal performance should always be one of their options. Think about what your ideal performance will look, feel, and sound like. If you are interviewing for that all-important job, sense, feel, and see yourself winning over your potential colleagues. When the ultimate version of success is happening, don't be surprised. Instead, stand by your excellence; it reflects your hard work and a well-developed performance plan. There will also be instances of bumpy performances, where you must scratch and claw your way to excellence. Be prepared through a quick review for a performance scenario where challenges are encountered and then overcome through your savvy intelligence and inner resourcefulness. You might have envisioned running the perfect road race only to encounter stomach or muscle cramps. These things are going to happen to you, as they do to the best of performers all the time. Be agile in advance of entering the ring and then once you enter to achieve your excellence. There are always environmental uncertainties and human factors; we are excellent, but no one is perfect. One saying I heard when I was an athlete was, "If you fail to plan, you plan to fail." You could achieve excellence by one of many potential scenarios, but even in a surprising scenario, there is logic waiting to be recognized and pressed into action. Have faith in your mental and physical reserves, and then tap into them.

Finally, there will come the time when the performance is in the books. Unlike most people who learn important lessons from transcending or just falling short, remember to document what you have learned about yourself, your preparation, your staffing, and your plan execution. Your task is always to learn from your performance lessons, to note them, and to ensure they become part of your evolving performance plan and the path to your next extraordinary performance. You have unique keys to performance just waiting to be unlocked and then picked up to open even more doors and applications of your gifts under pressure. Once you acquire a new lesson, a key of sorts, add it to your key chain so that you can unlock more doors, leading to more exciting opportunities.

Lesson Reminders

- Transcendence is meant to be a logical step forward once you have recognized a gift and worked with it for several months. Your application of the gift in a testing situation is a necessary step to gauge your current ability to apply it in a work, play, or personal life situation you have been aspiring to. Although enduring is important, you must approach rather than avoid testing of your gift.

- To transcend, you must stick to your performance plan, beginning with the weeks leading up to it. Part of your plan should include a review of what your unique plan should be. Then identify any lingering questions that might become larger if they are not examined and, when possible, resolve them. Sometimes a doubt will remain unresolved and must be carried with you into your opportunity to transcend. All people bring questions with them to their performances. Yours need to be brought down to their correct size, so that you know your strengths outweigh your current doubts.

- Within the final few days and hours leading to your performance, you are best served by sticking to a plan, where you focus on physical, emotional, and psychological recovery. Arrive at the performance fresh and sharp, not emotionally and physically flat. Although most people would agree with this premise, even Olympians tend to overtrain because they are insecure and feel as if they are grasping at the skills at their fingertips. Your best option is allowing the dust to settle after the challenging and systematic development of your gift. Only then can you think clearly and apply your gift to your best advantage when the time comes to transcend.

- When the time comes to perform, go with your skills, trust in them, and take a leap of faith and just perform. The hard work is in the bank; now it is time to cash in on your investment of time and energy and enjoy your gift. Throughout your quest to transcend, several possible scenarios will arise, including the best possible unfolding of your plan and ones that are more challenging. Remain in the present and work with your gift, given the scenario you are living out. Each transcendent performance is its own work of art. Having completed the process and endured, take the time to debrief your performance, learn from its lessons, recover, and then begin to plan for your next opportunity to transcend.

LESSON SEVEN
SYMMETRY

> *The desire for symmetry, for balance, for rhythm in form as well as in sound, is one of the most inveterate of human instincts.*
>
> Edith Wharton

I run outside in the fresh air most every day. My runs vary in distance from 10 to 30 kilometers depending on whether I am maintaining conditioning or building up to a road race, where length and speed become part of the qualities needed to transcend. The constant is that I run no matter the weather or temperature. Each run is its own clarifying experience, where body and mind reinvigorate and my perspective is restored. Runs are meditative opportunities used to work through the spectrum of challenges, emotions, and questions during each footfall in my life journey. The process of running, a rhythmic physical activity during which I speak only with myself, is something I crave, just like I crave a piping hot morning cup of coffee. While running, I reflect over the day and find overlooked pieces in my personal life, research projects, writing ideas, and strategies to use in my work with athletes, coaches, staff, and organizations. The parts of my life I am immersed in that day are considered, leading to important glimpses during each run. For example, I might realize that an important connection is missing on a chapter theme in my new book, one I didn't notice until part way through my run. Upon returning home, I jot down my new insights on a notepad while still in running clothes and then integrate the idea into the text once I am refreshed. During other runs I might think through a workplace challenge, such as how best to support a graduate student, deliver a student lecture, or work with colleagues. I might also find myself considering a much needed and improved approach to connect with a loved one. The running process is an activity that for me fosters a blend of equally important daily passions in a life performed well (69). Blending restorative activities into each day can offer creative opportunities to expand on ideas and resolve existing challenges through novel solutions you would not have thought of while in the thick of your workday. No one can spend all their time focused on a single pursuit or on a single part of what they do. Think back to the movie *Family Man* and how the main character came to realize he was much more than a business tycoon through an insightful glimpse into his potential before he ever chose to endure, transcend, and restore symmetry into his life.

A consideration of life blend, or symmetry, is an important lesson in terms of tapping into your gifts. Symmetry is about how effective you are in mixing your gifts into your daily and weekly existence. It takes more than a single gift to achieve a unique, personal sense of peace and harmony. Reflect on the words *harmony* and *blend*. Why are they important, and what do they suggest about how you can live and play with your gifts? For example, imagine that you are immersed in studying, working, or practicing your work or your sport. Someone walks into the room or phones you. You stop what you are doing for a second and look up. This important person wants to spend some time with you in what you first believe to be a moment when you are occupied. Does this person not notice, either by your facial expression, posture, or some other mannerism, that you are busy and becoming frustrated? Your energy is harnessed into a laser beam of focus and commitment, and you are being asked to stop what you are doing. You have traction in your activity and are making inroads on a task that is important to you. Despite being frustrated by the request, you look inward and decide you are being selfish. So, you quickly shift gears because you really like or love the person doing the asking. You have paused one pursuit to engage in another pursuit being proposed by someone important to you. Next, you take a few deep breaths and begin to engage with your family member or close friend in this other activity, and you recognize the excitement in their eyes. This person is excited not only by the activity but equally by your engagement in a shared moment. You value this person and so you play along, perhaps seeing yourself as a good sport. You feel benevolent and unselfish because you have put aside your gift pursuit. Then, before you even realize it, something magical is beginning to happen inside of you: the contagious sensation of pure fun and abandonment. This person or transitional circumstance has led you away from your singular focus and into another important part of you. You are being guided toward symmetry, perhaps through the engagement in valued relationships. Next, you are laughing and becoming increasingly attentive to the person you are playing with or the activity you are sharing. Fun is exactly what you needed to counterbalance your intensity, but you didn't know the transition was necessary for you to thrive until after the fact, once the activity of playing with your child, partner, or friend had ended (for now). They moved on, but the opportunity of the moment was captured because you chose wisely between two competing gifts, each a force unto itself. What can you learn from this scenario? Gifts are wonderful, but they should not be all consuming. When you make room for several gifts, there will be a symmetry in your day. What follows in this lesson is a challenge to the suggestion that being gifted requires singular investment in one activity.

Living With Multidimensional Commitment

Symmetry should not be associated with the term *balance*, meaning the precise balancing of a scale down to grains of sand. Symmetry, unlike balance, does not require perfect equivalence. Living one aspect of performance, such as your athleticism, employment, or a side project, is rewarding, but it is only part of who you need to be. Living in a healthy human condition is the only possible path to reinvigorating a gift you are pursuing. Why is symmetry important to you? Symmetry does more than help you develop a healthy perspective; it also ensures that as one application of a gift is waning, such as a professional career, you have prepared several places where you can redirect your energy. Symmetry fosters healthy life transitions. When one application fades, you simply substitute the old with newer applications of your gifts. Your life consists of many smaller parts such as diverse interests and passions, no matter your age, financial status, or education, and these diverse parts of you fuel and reinforce your multidimensional self (70). Your various gifts and the applications of them make you an interesting contributor to this world. As you thrive, you also touch the lives of other people in each gift pursuit instead of only one. You are much more than who you are as an athlete, lawyer, businessperson, educator, or scientist. Some people around you will believe it is wise to be totally committed in a single part of their life. They think of themselves as committed people and contrast their one-dimensional commitment with the unfocused characteristics of other people. The incorrect assumption is you can only do one thing at a time if you want to pursue it to the *n*th degree.

One-dimensional commitment is the place where many amateur and professional performers take a wrong turn in life, which eventually leads them to life crisis. A few renowned sport psychology professionals and I met for a series of world think tanks on athlete mental health (71). We have seen too many retired career professionals suffering from the poor strategy of an overprioritized dimension. These people, who must not include you, come to the recognition far too late in life that there is little left to do with their lives and no additional worth beyond the single dimension they no longer can pursue due to a worn-out body and mind. Persons committed to one domain are sort of like the major league baseball pitcher who gives his arm to the sport. When there is little to no mobility left in the arm, the baseball career is over. There has been an overinvestment in one part of life and an equally troubling underinvestment in others, such as family, friends, a new possible career, and a change in recreational activity. Each of your interests contributes to your life fulfillment, which then contributes to your capacity to endure and transcend when one part of your life has reached a logical end, such as an athletic career (72). At times in your life, you will feel as if you are pointing true north, meaning that you are traveling on your right path—the path where you will be content with how you are living and how you are choosing to blend your interests. At other times, you will lose your footing and feel as if you are on shaky ground without a compass and no visual access to the horizon—as if you are living in a thick fog. In some moments you've felt utterly lost, unable to see your next step or a bright future. I experienced such moments when leaving equestrian. When I was trying to complete my doctorate and the writing wasn't flowing no matter how many hours I sat in front of a flickering computer screen, I worried that if I didn't complete the degree, I would be nothing. During your precarious times, whether they are brief or long-lasting, you will experience the emotions and bodily sensations that come with uncertainty and confusion—fear or anger, an elevated heart rate, poor sleep, and unhealthy eating patterns. Your self-care will suffer. Whether you realize it or not, in the moment when you feel as if you are losing yourself, your feelings of impending loss and instability will be linked to a poor blending of priorities. You will have overemphasized one life aspect and neglected others; that is, a force is pulling you away from known aspects of your right path. You understand this concept having previously learned about competing forces, contortions, and glimpsed solutions. The competing forces of this world are tests asked of you daily as you engage with your gifts. How you choose to manage various gift opportunities needs to be a carefully thought-out decision each day, contributing to healthy blending and more life satisfaction.

Transitioning to New Gifts

You have several valuable gifts in need of daily attention. During one research study, I asked world-class performers about the breadth of their identities and how these equate with their contentment (73). Each of these dimensions needs to be protected and practiced daily, not only for today's symmetry but also to prepare you for inevitable future life transitions. Part of my responsibility as a mental performance consultant, in fact my favorite part, is the discussions with each athlete about their postcareer planning and next life steps. While my clients are ascending in their career, I propose that they can transport their well-honed training and performance skills—ambition, focus, relentless endurance, systematic planning, athleticism, intelligence, and handling pressure—to as many parts of their life as they choose. A considerable amount of knowledge is transferable in terms of the uptake of previous gifts that have been polished through life opportunities. The athlete can become a coach, motivational speaker, student, doctor, scientist, engaged family member, and much more, contingent on their interests. The teacher or professor can cultivate mentoring skills to engage with incoming educators or students or apply to a volunteer position. Anyone can also consult in and beyond their domain until they choose to no longer apply their gifts from their current profession. Each generation must always serve as sage guides to the next generation, giving what they know through time, effort, and knowledge to others like they once took from previous generations. Giving to others creates symmetry because it is a blending activity achieved by shifting your gaze from inside to outside the body. Mentoring will be your next and final lesson.

A certain grace and dignity exists when deciding when it is time to set aside one well-executed part of your life to make space for a better-chosen series of emerging interests, doing so on your own terms. I stepped down from being an equestrian, primarily because I no longer was excited by the lifestyle and time spent pursuing international events at the expense of other coveted gifts such as gaining a doctorate and a university position. I chose to transition into my new profession as a mentor to younger students and continued to work with aspiring athletes. I was fortunate in my choices because I could enjoy two treasured activities: sports and education. Although I initially thought my blend was correct because I pursued professional interests and had a flourishing personal life with my partner, I came to realize that my blend was not quite right. I had no hobbies to reinvigorate me, and my partner was not responsible to provide me with the answer of a best-suited recreational activity. I toyed inconsistently with running early in my academic and consulting careers. Because of a fortunate recognition that I was out of shape and carrying extra pounds, I needed to revisit my athlete identity sooner rather than later. The identity might have lurked in the shadows as I began carving out my professional career, but it was waiting in the wings as the key to what was missing from my life blend. Then came my glimpse (the run with my national team staff colleagues, with whom I could not keep up), followed by a dramatic shift in how I have since blended my time with several important gifts, not just an all-consuming professional career. Today, I am a successful national level master's half marathoner and a forever sports lover who is contemplating the possibilities of farther distances and faster times that naysayers regularly suggest to me are not possible. What I've learned in preparation for sporting events, I regularly apply in my mental preparation for the many public speeches and other important meetings in my schedule. My days are filled with being an athlete and endowed research chair, traveling to international destinations to support elite sport organizations and universities and, most important, by my family. Focusing on any one of these gifts in isolation would be a mistake and cause neglect of mind, body, family, and longevity. I am also now beginning to feel as if I have written in enough scientific journals, contributed substantively to the knowledge in my field, and traveled to sufficient international events, each one taking me away from my family and bringing me to living conditions best suited to younger bodies. So, my transitions continue to be smooth and graceful, and they are on my terms as opposed to being forced to transition because I've overstayed a welcome.

So, what am I trying to suggest to you? You are gifted in a variety of ways, and each gift can be applied to every part of your life as a novel application of a well-curated skill. Just as you are enjoying your immediate high-performance accomplishments using one gift, you must always attend to more current gifts to be healthy. Seed your future growth and build new pastures in which to play and thrive. I learned as a boy living on a farm that a single field is not meant to remain fertile indefinitely, just as you are much more than the athlete or professional person. You are a family member and a friend; you have personal interests and gifts with untapped potential. The objective must be to remain a searcher, always listening and recognizing new ways and places to apply the characteristics and talents that magnify your giftedness. A life well-lived is one lived in symmetry. Living in symmetry means you are open and always in the process of reinvention while keeping hold of the golden thread that weaves through your life. You are uniquely talented and gifted in many more ways than one.

So why wait another day to consider your symmetry? Stop what you are doing right now and consider the parts of your life you have pressed into action so far. What have you been chipping away at? Have you been working on a specific project? What must you do today to secure a healthy blend of interests and gifts for tomorrow and the future? Just as you need to work, you also need to play and remain interesting, for your sake and the sake of those who love you. There is much more to you than meets the eye, even your current eye. Almost every regret I have heard has come from someone living a life without sufficient blend. The cost to these people and their loved ones is immense, short-sighted, and neglectful. Lives are blown up because of a lack of symmetry; a gifted person is dissatisfied yet has taken no action to grow and expand their horizon. Be much more than a gifted employee, sportsperson, or business owner. These parts of you are temporary and open to negotiation and change, sometimes on short notice. You cannot regain a day banked to time, lost in the confines of a singular task such as writing, balancing a ledger, or fine-tuning your sports skills. However, the days ahead of you are each one as important as those already banked, assuming you listen to existing forces, current contortions, and recent glimpses. Begin to plan for up-and-coming evolutions that will add to your life quality through symmetry.

Prioritizing Self-Care

Your body and mind will undergo wear and tear and some elevated stress load as you continue to evolve into who you are meant and built to be. Stress load is unavoidable when healthy change is being sought. Rest and recovery must become an essential part of your daily routine no matter what experience you have banked that day. You must reboot. Eat well, allow sufficient time to wind down each day, reflect, learn, and sleep well. Only then can you launch into the next day with a clear mind and a healthy progressive orientation. Even with Olympic athletes living out their lives at a Herculean level, sport scientists and motivators working with these people know from compelling evidence that more than 50 percent of high-performance athletes are sleep deprived because their minds are still on the job. Compounded into their lives is imbalance caused by overworking and overpursuing their dreams in those waking hours, to the point where far too many performers exist in a perpetual state of physical and psychological strain, leading to foreseeable burnout (74). Self-care is a much more important concern than performers amid their pursuits recognize—they overtrain without sufficient recovery, and often believe they are immortal, until they aren't (75). I find it fascinating (though never surprising) when world-class athletes struggle with their self-care considering their exacting expectations, sensory self-awareness, and outstanding capacity to act on their visions. They are consumed with living out their dreams with passion and fighting with intensity to capture their desires. In this process, most extraordinary performers falter at some point (as you might have done), and then they either efficiently or inefficiently correct their choices and return to symmetry or lose their ability to act on any of their gifts. When a person is exhausted and neglectful of their body and mind, excellence is not possible.

You have basic needs that must be met each day, cumulatively over time, before you can function at your best and sustain excellence. You would be surprised how often interpersonal issues and internal struggles are resolved when you take time in your day for a healthy snack, exercise, social balance, other fun activities, and sufficient sleep—each, an often-neglected antidote to stress. When children grow hungry, they are usually fed; yet adults are much more neglectful of themselves. To take time away from a gift pursuit might not be easy for you, just as it is not easy for Olympians and professional athletes (76). However, you must set down your pursuit at certain points each day and enjoy that cup of tea, coffee, wine, whiskey, time with family, or a run (or walk) with a friend or your dog. When you forget about self-care, you are choosing to ignore your mind and your body, and you are also underestimating the consequences of your choices. Glimpses are meant to help you restore symmetry, but as previously mentioned, they often go unheard or are rationalized away as inopportune, resulting in lost time and self-compromise.

When you engage in healthy blending as your life mission, you are doing more than safeguarding against the compromise of a single coveted gift. Every world-class performer needs to have enough blending in their daily life to succeed in the present. The performer must also set a clear and promising horizon worthy of exploration and investment or risk being compromised when the gift becomes smaller. Each day, as you see others lose precious time to asymmetry, whether their decision is deliberate or not, pause and think about your pathway. You have a promising present, which must be full of splendid gifts in place of one lonely and overemphasized gift. The athlete can be an Olympic or world champion, and the capture of such an experience is remarkable. But equally important is the time they spend away from their gift and how they choose to spend it. Whether you are an Olympian or a family member, you must be an overall interesting person. Continue to develop several gifts that interest you so that life in the present and the future remains exciting rather than repetitive. If you are open to more of your gifts, you also prepare for a brighter horizon where many treasured opportunities will be explored, discovered, and brought to reality.

Action Item Seven: Making Decisions About Gifts in Your Life

High-level performers often become exceptional in a specific part of their life. To remain in a state where you are thriving, your life needs to be symmetrical, meaning the diverse gifts in your life need to be cultivated regularly. Being symmetrical in relation to gifts means you transfer the gifts in one part of your current and future life to others. If your gifts include being a great leader, you can lead in your workplace and a volunteer organization. Leadership skills also speak to another complementary gift: you like to inspire other people. You might also have further gifts that only require your own inspiration, such as an interest in a sport or hobby. All kinds of gifts together make up your gift potential. What gifts contribute to your symmetry? Open your laptop or grab a piece of paper and pen. The first item on the list is an easy one to write—likely it is the activity you are working toward and enduring with right now. There will always be a gift at the forefront of your mind. Here comes the challenge: Dig a little deeper and see what further gifts you have. Some of these might only gain a little time investment now, and others have been purposefully put on the back burner. Then, think back to gifts you once used that were strategically abandoned, meaning you chose not to continue with them. Look through the list you have developed—it's probably lengthier than you first anticipated. Which of these gifts is past its prime (label as "past due")? Which gifts are overripe (label as "overripe")? Are any gifts nearing their logical conclusion (label as "nearing conclusion")? How about the gifts that are bearing fruit right now (label as "ripe")? Are any of your gifts under development but in early days (label as "emerging")? Finally, have you glimpsed any gifts that you need to seed sometime soon because they are part of your wish list (label as "wish list")? Each of these gifts is part of your giftedness, with some needing to be identified as past their due date, some regarded as still highly nourishing, some emerging, some nearing the assembly line and being packaged up for use, and some farther on the horizon. Take a few minutes to identify what classification belongs with each gift. You can do this task.

Now that you have looked through your gifts, make a few important decisions using the provided labeling terms. Start with those requiring strategic abandonment. Look at some of those gifts that served you so well and gifted you and many others over the years. For example, one of your gifts might have been an amazing intensity you could bring to the courtroom as a litigator. Another person's gift might have been the ability to lead a research team in the medical sciences. A third person's gift would have been the ability to ride horses, box, run marathons, or play professional tennis. All these people inevitably move beyond their prime in the use of their gift, at least when it comes to performance. At some point, these gifts are holding you back. You can no longer sustain the energy required to do them to the top level. Therefore, it's time for you to develop a dignified exit strategy as opposed to digging in and setting yourself up for an inevitable decline after which you are disregarded. Develop an exit strategy for one such gift, one you are using only because it is something that has served you well in the past. Remember, there is a time to harvest what you've planted, and there is also a time to change fields and cultivate new land.

There is little reason to focus on a gift that is still bearing fruit. However, what you might consider is a time line to its use. Every ripe item has a due date before which it can be consumed and after which its quality and taste diminish. Therefore, work with your gifts that are fruitful, but set an approximate time line to reexamine its fruitfulness and whether its yield is still at the highest level, where your gift is magnificent and enjoyable. Return to your well-developed gifts every six months and reexamine them. This sort of reflective process will confirm you are still on track with a bountiful gift or reveal if the quality of the gift is becoming compromised. Decide whether you must revise the way you are working with the gift or whether it is due for strategic abandonment, much as world-renowned boxer Lennox Lewis stepped away from his sport when he was still a world champion but beginning to feel tired. A gift bearing fruit but on the decline might be repurposed to a new use. I recall a fantastic boxer who was known in youth as a knockout artist. The boxer originally relied on speed and power to best opponents. As the boxer became older, I noticed a change in style. He was still a gifted boxer but no longer fought at a long distance where he could really throw a punch and at the same time risk being punched at full force. Instead, the boxer became what is known as an inside fighter. The fights were at a close distance where the boxer didn't have to rely on as much movement, speed, and power. He went on to capture many world titles with his revised style of fighting, which now included ring savvy in place of skills he relied on when younger. Similarly, you can revise the way you tap into your gift, providing there is a way to revise your style and providing you still have a love of the gift. For example, a now deceased family member was a world-class salesperson. During his youth, he sold his products in high volume. The effort required long days and short nights. As he aged, he considered whether the stamina required for volume sales was possible. The conclusion was that my family member could no longer sustain selling merchandise on the floor, in high volume. The refined strategy was to sell only boutique-level products to the select few aficionados. The revenue continued, as did the love of selling. What changed was the strategy. If you decide to continue to pursue your gift, refine your strategy to match your current physical and mental stamina as well as your family demands. Otherwise, you will stay beyond your current ripened state. So, your challenge is to decide which of the two pathways to choose: setting an end date or revising how the gift is used for the near future.

Another gift scenario for you to consider is the exciting possibilities inherent in the gift that is only a seed now. What seed of an idea have you been thinking about? If some strategic abandonment is already in process, there is some room opening in your schedule to explore a new and exciting possibility. When I reduced the amount of time traveling the world with amateur athletes, something I could have clung onto as some colleagues tend to do, time opened to write this book. I have always thought there was more to writing and thinking than only producing scientific peer-reviewed articles. Although I enjoy writing to an academic audience, I had begun to sow this new seed of writing to a non-academic audience. People are important to me, and for many years I had no time to reach out and write to a lay audience. But the moment has arrived, and I am seeding a new skill. When I submitted the first draft of what I thought was a wonderful book to literary agents, it was far from the mark. I didn't yet understand the difference between writing to an academic reader and someone who lives, works, and plays outside of university settings. Then I was fortunate enough to secure the editorial support I now have. The feedback from my first draft was eye-opening. I am learning an immense lesson in how to translate thinking into writing, and through the writing, suggesting to the reader how to translate thinking into doing. I am seeding this new area of my life, and it is exciting. There is a new idea, very much out of the box, germinating because of this book and the exchanges I am having in the refinement of ideas about the eight lessons to giftedness. The bottom line is that letting go of past-due gifts opens you up to new and exciting gifts, which in turn will provide you with positive energy and further meaning in your life. Therefore, if you are closing one chapter in your giftedness, seed a new one. Identify the seed kernel, develop a plan of action, and follow the endurance lesson spelled out in lesson five.

Take the time to work through the sorts of gifts you have classified. Then, make the important and necessary decisions for you to progress in your gifts. Progression helps you remain engaged with life and the important people around you. Change is inevitable; look at your changes as evolution, not loss.

Lesson Reminders

- ❖ You can choose to live each day with symmetry or asymmetry. You must commit to a wise blend of gifts as opposed to chasing down only one. You have many gifts, and drawing upon your diversity of gifts will bring you happiness and perspective, whereas drawing on only one gift can compromise your gift pursuit and long-term happiness.

- ❖ Try to extend your pursuit of gifts to several areas that can add to your potential as a person. You might like competing in individual sports, teaching, litigating, or operating a business. All these pursuits are wonderful places to be gifted and to thrive. Stretch yourself by working on other areas of your life that will also add meaning, such as cooking for family and working on personal relationships. You need to be gifted at several things at once to thrive.

- ❖ There is a method to enjoying a gift during a lengthier existence. You cannot sustain indefinitely the pursuit of one gift, especially not in the form where it first rewarded you. People evolve, and so too must the uptake of their gifts by drawing upon other equally important gifts. Consider the athlete with a certain style of play built around youth and speed over experience. Gifts coming from your body are expected to be prioritized, and so you rely on strength, stamina, and rapid-fire intuition. When an athlete evolves in a sport, it is because the gift intertwines with other gifts that are different from those tapped in youth, such as wisdom, experience, and patience. Symmetry even in relation to a single gift, then, requires the use of other talents and experiences as support.

❖ Symmetry requires you to examine gifts and make important decisions about which ones stay and which ones must soon be let go. Look at your gifts as temporary. You might extend their use by evolving your style of play, but each gift has a time and place in your life course. Plan for the day when a gift will either lose its appeal or strength and power. The best strategy is to identify the gifts you presently know about and begin to anticipate when one is overly ripe and ready for strategic abandonment. Those that are yielding quality fruit should continue to evolve but not be counted on as indefinite—they too will become past due at a certain point. So, you must continue to develop newer gifts as you entertain possible future explorations that match with your lifestyle and time demands.

THE EDUCATOR-MENTOR

Summer is over and autumn classes are beginning. The professor and mental performance consultant is now an established educator and mentor and has returned from another major international sporting event. His approach has become seasoned over many years, first as an athlete, then as a supporter of excellence. Facing this year's students, he begins his speech, setting the stage for a teaching and learning exchange the students have not yet heard or experienced. Over the years, many students have arrived at the professor's courses, armed and ready with pen and paper to take the mandatory notes, fulfill traditional assignments, and jump through necessary hoops. The goal in the students' minds is to complete this course, much like the courses before, and gain a grade, preferably of a higher score. The students shuffle into the class and find the professor sitting calmly on top of a desk, waiting patiently for the final one to straggle in. The room door is then shut. There is a tension spurred by the unknown. What will this professor want? What sort of person will the students need to contort into? The professor lets the silence of the moment sink in and wash over the class as the students wait a little longer for their questions to be answered, for the professor to speak. Until they know the path through this hoop—his course—an uncertainty lingers.

The professor feels and sees the questioning in the eyes and postures of the learners before him—they are momentarily caught short. He thinks back to a time when he was a student and someone else stood and taught. His recollection traces back to a power differential lorded over him and his classmates by a stern and unfriendly educator. Perhaps this very power differential is exactly what the students are expecting—that is, to be relegated to the role of subordinates. Their world is about to turn on its axis. He smiles and begins to speak in a calming tone with a cadence unfamiliar to the students. The professor is not speaking at them or to them, he is dialoguing with them. A new form of student–educator relationship is at its beginning. The students do not know it yet, but they are in for quite a ride. The professor's tone is infused with passion, fun, and something else the students cannot yet put their fingers on, perhaps daring. Then suddenly a recognition dawns in their eyes; they are being invited to embark on an adventure and to suspend a mindset typically oriented to outcome. The professor knows the students are torn. They wish for closure and certainty. Part of them still wishes for the conventional, but the conventional is not to be. They need to adapt to a very different role.

While the students embark on their journey, the professor traces back to his own educational experience, to a high school teacher who invited learning and critical thinking. What he wanted from the students before him was a dialogue in which students could place learning over results and where there were many places at the table for open discussion and individual thinking. The key to this course is simple and yet difficult. The students need to be themselves. They need to share their thinking, and they need to summon confidence that what they will offer will be sufficient. Soon enough they will come to realize their views are relished in this sacred classroom. Soon the students will encourage one another instead of competing. They will begin to think about what they really wish to learn from this teacher and each other, a question they may never have asked in earlier courses. Certainly, part of what they will learn will relate to the course content. However, there is another deeper dimension to the course. The professor wants the students to rediscover their curiosity and learn how to learn as a process. What they have to say and what they will discuss is important. *How* they will engage in their discussions is yet more important.

Within three classes the students have transcended beyond their concern of course outcome—grades are all but forgotten. They are dialoguing freely with the professor and each other as respected colleagues. They each arrive at the class with a warm coffee or tea in hand and maybe a snack to nibble on. With each successive class, the students become more engaged. Occasional student absences are necessary, but they are felt to be losses by the students and by the professor. Knowledge has also begun to include an understanding of how to relate based on who the student is and how she or he wishes to share ideas with the rest of the group. The professor sees this transformation, reminding him of another glimpse from his past. This time he channels lessons gifted by the wise chief who touched his life and altered his way of thinking and doing from the moment they met when he was a young career professional. The students are learning the difference between what they are and who they are.

With each passing week, the course moves too rapidly toward its logical conclusion. The students are sad. They feel a sense of loss because this experience—a process in place of an outcome—

could have continued for another term, buying them more time to reconnect with the concept of shared learning and self-discovery. During a quiet moment in the second-to-last class of the term, one student first looks at the professor with a gleam in her eye and then speaks. She proposes writing a book to share the process she and her colleagues have undergone with a wider audience. She believes the lesson and path to being oneself is important and rarely achieved in a teaching and learning environment. The professor says little, his cheeks warming with a blend of humility and pride, as his mind races. On the one hand, the students have captured the essence of this class. The professor wonders how the journey (a process) has ironically turned to the production of yet another outcome, when the intended lesson was to be for the present moment. On the other hand, extraordinary outcomes always develop from healthy, immersive, and authentic processes, not from mundane living. As the student persists with her pitch, it is the professor's turn to be caught short. The professor begins to glimpse a new way to explore his journey of tapping into his gifts as creative thinker, educator, and performer—by putting the ideas shared with his classmates into written words previously espoused to world-class athletes and students, but never inked. In this way the rediscovery of the professor's desire to write personally (not just as a scientist and scholar)—a desire formed before the launch into an academic position—is rekindled. Once again, a vast horizon is arrayed before the author and he feels somewhat uncertain, just as all people do, when they embark on a journey not yet traveled.

This story reflects a transitional point for this author, just as it is meant to be transitional for you. We all find ourselves playing various roles each day and across weeks, months, and years, sometimes as a learner and sometimes as a teacher focused on regifting to others. We are never exclusively confined to one of these roles over the other. As we teach, we also continue to learn, which in turn, improves what and how we support those around us. As we encourage other people to explore their possibilities, we will often find ourselves in new, uncharted territories of our own making; discussions with others remind us that we also have a path to forge. The lessons we gained from earlier explorations and growth can always be tapped as we continue in life, looking for new ways to harness our energy and potential. In many instances throughout life we may believe we have reached our apex, just as someone who achieves an Olympic status or wins a world championship has. If there is anything a healthy life education offers, it is the inevitability that there will always be yet another monumental summit in waiting, one that will call to you if you choose to listen and then act. We are never just teacher or student; we are both.

LESSON EIGHT
REGIFTING

In teaching others, we teach ourselves.

Traditional Proverb

Gifts are precious and need to be nurtured for your life to be completely fulfilled. When you opt not to tap into your gifts, at least some of what lies in wait for you is frustration and a sense of underachievement. Reflecting on the words and ideas from the previous seven lessons, you have identified, revisited, refined, and begun or improved upon the application of your gifts in the areas and stages of a well-lived and satisfying life. As you continue your path forward by embracing your giftedness in its different forms, you will evolve at a rapid pace, one you might not have even hoped for. You must commit to mapping out and then embarking on exciting new adventures over the course of your life, which will then add to your vibrancy and enthusiasm in place of sitting still and becoming dissatisfied with your life's meaning. One final piece to the gifting journey is the importance of gifting back to the people whose lives you touch, so they can forge healthy paths, just like yours. The term *regifting* is often associated with packaging up a gift you previously received from someone else, perhaps as a holiday or birthday present, and finding it a new home. People sometimes regift bottles of wine, clothing, cologne or perfume, sports apparel, board games, and gift cards. Although regifting can be associated with the rehoming of a material possession that does not suit you to someone who might find a better use for it, there is a second meaning of the term in relation to this book and our discussion. Regifting is about paying forward the key gifting lessons you have learned on your journey, so more people can be encouraged to tap into their gifts, develop them, and work and play to their best and most natural strengths within their unique life circumstances. These gifts you choose to pay forward might be teaching a technical skill to a student such as, for example, a former elite athlete, who then becomes a coach to the next generation of athletes, or a medical intern who becomes a resident, then an experienced professional, and then a supervising physician who mentors newly minted physicians.

Regifting might have less to do with your area of expertise and more to do with supporting a healthy pathway toward another person's gifts by way of process, such as when you help guide someone else in setting a vision, persistence, leadership, communication, or collaboration. The essential point is to share the best skills and processes you have learned, just as other special people have helped you find the way to your gifts. I have witnessed legendary athletes giving not only their knowledge but also their creativity to the next generation of athletes. I have also been personally invested in helping forge the next generation of sport psychology researchers and international societal leaders. As was clarified in lesson seven, when one of our gifts wanes, or even when we are in the thick of a gift still bearing its fruit, we need to give back what we have taken from the earth. Otherwise, sustained growth of a broader ecological system of human potential will falter because gifts in the form of seeds have not been sown for others to also harvest. People must thrive, and it is our human responsibility to help others develop to their potential, as some people have supported us. And so, the final lesson in this book must be about how to share gifts with others, to help them, while also reinforcing another application of your gifts by giving of yourself.

Regifting Is a Win–Win Situation

Let me contextualize the lesson by sharing a story with you that was touching to be part of and thought provoking to witness. It was a gifting exchange between two very special people. Several years ago, I worked with a world-renowned athlete preparing for an epic sport event. The athlete, a wise student of his chosen sport, approached a stranger (his sport idol) who was an epic athlete and historical figure—one of the greats of all time. When my client approached the coaching staff and indicated he was going to seek out his former idol to join the team, there was some initial resistance and feelings among some on the team of being undermined. The person being approached was not known to be a coach and was also several years past the glory days when he made his name and became a legendary icon. What followed was fascinating to the entire support team, none of whom knew the potential addition by anything other than reputation as a former athlete. A few weeks later, the team converged in a warm location for a training camp, where the new staff member joined us. He quickly became a well-liked member in the house we were sharing temporarily in a training camp environment. The lingering question was whether this new addition could parlay a monumental athletic history and bank of personal experience into a regifting process, where my client could learn and then apply refined skills in a short amount of time against a renowned and popular opponent. Motivational consultants know the power of learning from extraordinary others through their experiences, termed *vicarious learning*, which they in turn can help us parlay into first-hand skills to build our competence and self-confidence (77). At first, the training camp proceeded as most such camps typically do, with people finding their natural places in the team. Coffee was made in the morning by one person. One person would vacuum the house, and another would shop; these were our informal roles that helped unify the team and improve our shared living condition. We all carried our formal roles as well, such as coach, assistant coach, mental performance consultant, nutritionist, strength and conditioning professional, and massage therapist. The head coach structured the days, assigned the training partners, and the rest of us were always in attendance, filling our roles and supplementing support when asked by either the head coach or the athlete.

Within a few days, the camp structure began to soften as the team began to gel, found its rhythm, and we pulled in the same direction, with a unified vision of the athlete transcending. The former athlete and icon, now a technical and tactical consultant in the team, spoke increasingly with the athlete and coach about the opponent, bringing forward creative ideas based on our client's style and the opponent's liabilities. There are many ways people can be regifted with knowledge, either through dialogue, visually, by example, or in this case, the athlete sought a combination of visual and hands-on learning and simulations (78). The retired athlete began his gifting process with informal demonstrations of potential tactics. Then he began to role play with the younger athlete, first in slow motion, all the while talking through his reasoning with the athlete, coaches, and mental performance coach. The icon understood we all had to unite and reinforce the same message to the athlete for it to be absorbed and applied when transcendence was required. By the third week, and increasingly from that point in the camp through to performance day when the athlete transcended to yet another monumental accomplishment, the two athletes—one regifting enthusiasm and creativity, the other being gifted—played out the sport by the hour, enjoying each other's company and the strategies being rehearsed. They were immersed in a shared passion for their sport, a passion often lost in professionals who slip past their workdays. The camp became increasingly jovial as the entire team became wrapped up in regifting, each playing a unique but interconnected part in a creative process we knew would be epic due to the richness and unorthodoxy of what was playing out. Next, we transitioned from our training camp location to the city where the sporting event was going to be featured. The mentor and his protégé remained tight as the days wound down and continued in their play and discussions about tactics and what they were seeing most recently in terms of the opponent's emotional response as the event was within a few days. On the day of the performance, the athlete, the former athlete, and I went for an afternoon walk in the large city where the performance later took place in front of a sold-out, standing-room-only coliseum. The walk was scheduled to remind the young athlete that he was among people and not alone in those final hours. Isolation is the enemy of human connection, which is needed in the regifting process. The athlete would have to feel connected with the persuasive support from his staff and the audience to feel even more purpose in his mission toward transcendence (79). When our walk and talk around the city streets came to an end, the two athletes naturally began one final game of playing tactics outside the hotel, both continuing to have fun, both in the moment enjoying their respective roles and each other's company. The outcome later that night was foreseeable, given the generosity of the mentor to share knowledge and the generosity of the protégé to invite the retired athlete into his team. To this day the performance is hard to describe without the accompaniment of video images, lighting, and the sounds from the crowd. The athlete entered the arena to cheers and naysayers, standing shoulder to shoulder, with more naysayers than cheers because the opponent was the fan favorite. Then came the revealing of the gift, human transcendence, as it was efficiently unwrapped and opened in front of the electrified audience. Within the first two minutes of an hour-long performance, all resistance against my client dissipated as people, including my client's opponent, were displaced to the role of accepting his greatness on worldwide television, accompanied by a collective chanting of his name.

This story is one of grace and dignity. The former champion and hero recognized excellence in the athlete being regifted and supported the younger person, whose time had come to create a performance that reflected the very best version of the current athlete and not any semblance of the retired athlete other than a shared attitude toward creativity and discovery through play. Although it is easy to reinvent another person as oneself and believe we are graciously transferring our wisdom to the next generation, there is a certain skill and process to sharing what we have learned from our own steps and missteps. The person sharing wisdom or expertise needs to recognize the person they are supporting is someone entirely their own, with the right to free will as opposed to contortion. Every performer has a personal gift and a unique way of adapting that gift based on their body, mind, and chosen application of creativity. Many a coach or teacher attempts to create clones in their protégés. You and I have watched an educator or employer try to re-create themselves in the people who surround them, so all think, talk, look, and even dress as they do. Although copying another person is a form of flattery for the person being copied (the person meant to be regifting), there is a second side to the story of emulating or being asked to emulate another person. The person being copied is flattered and personally reinforced but is not supporting the recipient's ingenuity, uniqueness, and personhood. Instead, the mentor is opting away from gifting the other and is affirming the duplication of their own chosen path. The assumption of the person regifting is that all people want to walk a path just like theirs, and that their path makes sense across people.

Can you think of a time when you were either the recipient or the person doing the regifting? What was your process like? If you were the one gifting, did you try to guide your protégé to walk the same path you did, in the same way, or did you encourage them to travel their own path in their own way? What sort of exchange, knowing what you know now about regifting, should have happened as compared with what did happen? If you were the person being gifted, what was your reaction when the person regifting was sharing their gift but, in exchange, expected you to adopt their style and approach when taking up the gift? You know the answer to each of these questions, many of which cannot end in long-term success. Sometimes the person will want to learn your gift and walk a path like yours, given that the pathway is well tested and seems to be effective. If this is the case, be prepared—they will at a certain point also want to develop their own unique twist in terms of how they set their path and reach for their gift. Remember, your role is gifting, but what the other person does with the gift once it is theirs is a choice only they should make. You might think you know best how to use a gift you are sharing, but each person is unique and no two pathways toward gifts can ever be the same. People are unique in their backgrounds, values, personality, and physical makeup.

Circling back to the two boxers, there was also a second part to the gifting process the two storied athletes underwent that can add further depth to this lesson of regifting. The obvious gift was the one gained by the protégé from the more experienced icon. However, the gifting process is never meant to be unidirectional. The person receiving the gift is not just a passive recipient when it comes to learning from a more seasoned mentor. The protégé is also opened to learning, and amid becoming the learner and expanding on a personal gift, is creating a venue for the more experienced person doing the regifting to share what has been learned and remains of value. The sharing exchange confirms the mentor's knowledge and wisdom, reminding that person their gift is alive and well, just in an altered application that matches the mentor's current developmental moment. The athlete will not always remain in the role of athlete, just as the frontline salesperson will not be able to sustain the frenetic pace needed to be at the top of their game. Instead of being stuck in a past application, there is always the possibility of a new and exciting opportunity to pass on your gift to someone else if you are willing.

Beyond wanting to unselfishly support others in their pursuit of excellence, why should you be motivated to regift your knowledge and expertise to other people? When you regift you are encouraged to contemplate how you realized your own gifts and the prized road you took to get there. Reminders of past choices and actions are important, not to belabor the steps and missteps you experienced but instead to solidify the positive steps you took on your journey and remind you how the journey was of tremendous value. Skills mature and then they evolve. I used to treasure leading scientific publications and pulling others along. Now, I lead from the back, pushing others forward, as their mentor. Therefore, any opportunity to revisit your pathway and retrace your steps in the quest to help someone else can also further cement your healthiest path forward by serving as an ongoing reminder of where you once were and how it links meaningfully with where you are now and where you intend to go next. Regifting is a win–win situation, with people experiencing important growth.

Developing Your Regifting Process

How can you develop a regifting process? What sorts of gifts can you offer a potential gift recipient? Imagine you are a parent looking to regift experiences to one of your own children or a close relative. You might love running and experience a certain giftedness when engaging in your preferred physical activity. The person before you might not have any interest in running at all. You might have tried to run with this person, but within a few days you were met with resistance or disinterest. The person engaged in the activity but showed no commitment to it because it wasn't fun. Should you continue to push the concept of running or reconsider how your skills might apply to another activity more exciting to the person? Far too many people looking to regift push their chosen activity on someone else, only to discover the person is disinterested in the gift you wrapped for them, at least for the time being. Think of a situation when you tried to engage someone in an activity or job task you were extremely passionate about because you thought it would bring further value and mobility to them if they learned it. Remember, just as you experienced competing forces (discussed in lesson two), the person you are wanting to share your gift with will also experience competing forces.

Step one is to identify a person you think might benefit from the gift you have wrapped and are ready to give. For the person to benefit from the gift, you must consider whether the person has the potential to be gifted in the area you are considering before ever making your approach. Step two, if you believe the intended recipient has a hidden gift you can help with, you must ask this person whether they have any interest in the gift you are looking to share; that is, have they glimpsed it as being part of their future? Considering what you learned in lesson three, are you asking the person to contort or is the offering of your gift an action that truly aligns with the person's path as they envision it? A careful and open discussion should be had between you and the potential recipient to find out whether they would be pleasing you or themselves if the decision is to proceed and receive the gift. The discussion will take you to step three, where you and this person will share the glimpses their potential and be excited by it, such as we discussed in lesson four. From the glimpsing process, you will both know within a short period of time (such as within the day) whether your offer is an idea the recipient wishes to seed at this time. Surely, you could recall times when people might have offered to teach you a certain skill, such as how to debate, camp outdoors, sell a product, or some other activity they loved. You needed to decide if that activity was appealing to you, and if it was, whether this was the time to engage. Part of the regifting process is that you can offer someone a gift. Once you have offered a gift, the person must be allowed to decide for themselves whether to receive it and subsequently choose to open it up and explore its meaning. Never be offended by someone else's chosen path when you offer to share your gifts; the offering alone reinforces generosity and an additional asset—looking beyond yourself to support someone else on their path.

On one occasion, I was the person looking to mentor someone through my gift as an educator and researcher. There was a young student who chose to pursue studies in my research lab who I knew had a tremendous potential to learn. The student was open in discussion and was the sort of potential candidate who belongs in the helping profession in which I work, at the highest level. I have supported many high-quality graduate students who've studied sport psychology at the master's and doctoral levels. I am prepared to invest thousands of hours in a student, but my time does not even come close to the hours that my students commit to their learning pursuits. Some of the students who completed their doctorates chose to do what was necessary to complete their degrees, but even I knew they were not fully unwrapping their gift of becoming an internationally recognized scholar–practitioner, a gift I was looking to encourage. One student was at a crossroad in a master's degree. I knew the student was bright and had at least as much potential, if not more, as I had starting out. The question before both of us was: Did this person wanted to be fully committed to learning all the skills needed to become an exceptional educator and scholar, or would the degree suffice? One fine morning the student and I sat in my research lab and looked through the window at the beautiful lake nearby. The student had just completed that day's summer job commitments and was back at the computer churning out the studies needed to complete a master's degree. "What does your future look like?" I asked. While the student reflected on the question, I explained there was a crossroad before them. One path would be the successful completion of the master's degree, which could include publishing and practical mentoring working with athletes but no further benefits. The second option would include an immersive experience and open the student up to a doctoral scholarship, the doctorate itself, high-volume publishing in international journals, and the subskills that would take this person to a well-paying international work position. There was no quick answer to my question; the student needed to return home to think about the proposal for a few days, discuss it with family, and then decide whether the gift being offered was something the person valued and glimpsed as their bright future. No matter how much I wanted the student to decide in favor of my gift offer, I could not push this person to accept what was being offered. I had tried encouraging a few half-committed students, like half-committed athletes in the past, and it never was rewarding for the person regifting or the one receiving. In this case, the student did return to me with an immediate response of ignited enthusiasm. The student had conferred with family the night before, and they encouraged the student to chase down the gift being offered. Our next step was to develop a workable plan, like the structuring unpacked in lesson five about endurance. The gift recipient has touched upon transcendent experiences many times since accepting the gift offer by publishing in renowned scientific journals, coteaching graduate-level courses, and working with aspiring athletes. This outcome was a success story, but not all gift offerings turn out as we hope. All you can do is offer your time and your gift, and by offering, you are choosing the healthy pathway forward of regifting.

Other regifting possibilities can also lead to a success story. Not every gift you might have to offer is a hard skill, such as knowledge in a sport discipline or an employment skill. In some cases you will see the opportunity to regift a soft skill, such as helping to develop a preexisting gift visible in someone else but requiring polish, like group leadership, effective communication, or even how to endure in a gift pursuit. So, the person standing before you might wish to endure at an activity or a gift glimpsed that is different from one of the gifts you cultivated on your path. What then?

My oldest son has embraced karate, a sport I never tried and only have worked with in a consulting role. The event that opened his opportunity to the sport happened by accident. I was walking into my university one day and met up with an old friend who was teaching an activity course on karate. I mentioned my son's innate tendency to play wrestle, grapple, punch, and kick, all parts of how we play fight together. The coach suggested I bring my son for two trial sessions at his dojo. When I mentioned the idea to my son, he was immediately enthusiastic. It has been several years since I first started driving him to karate lessons, and I have attended most of his sessions and every belt exam along his exciting journey. I know little about karate first-hand, and yet I am now riveted by his progression and curiosity in his chosen activity. He plays with his karate by blocking attacks when we play fight, and he has become much faster than me with his reflexes. I literally cannot touch him when we goof around as he easily blocks all my attempts. All I can do in these humorous moments is laugh at his proficiency and my awkwardness of movement. What I offer is support and transportation to and from my son's training and I encourage his gift pursuit when inevitably he experiences challenging sessions or becomes discouraged. The regifting in this case is one of supporting someone else I care about in their chosen activity by reinforcing his endurance and passion. At the same time, I do know something about how to chase down a dream, and so I support my son in the process of chasing down his. He is learning a life lesson beyond karate skills and colorful belts of how to work through challenges and come out the other side.

We each bring to the table our own interests and choices of how to apply our gifts. My younger son has also chosen a sport uniquely to his own liking—basketball. People you are choosing to regift to might not want to take you up on becoming the next generation of your gift. They have a plan of their own, one they hopefully glimpse and chase down. You might be a successful business owner, but someone else might wish to pursue employment in an organization and work their way upward, but not to ownership. You can regift many things. Listen carefully to the person you are wanting to help before determining the type of gift you should offer. As we discussed already, your task as the person regifting is not to create a clone but to encourage someone to pursue their gifts and support them either through hard skills or soft skills, as each fits best. People hold a diversity of gifts, and there is a time and place where they choose to tap these. Your version of giving back must be in the form of support and it must align with an opportunity they wish to seed.

So, what have you learned from this brief discussion on regifting? Every person has their own unique gifts. You are continuing a path that includes chasing down your own glimpses and turning them into reality. Just as you pursue gifts for yourself, the people around you are on their own individual paths. You and those around you are each entitled to pursue your own gifts in time. Some of the gifts you pursue in a lifetime are eventually in your past, some are in your present, and some are in your near or distant future. Some opportunities that people suggest to you are not a great fit. You instinctively know these generous offers not to be a good fit with who you are and who you wish to become. Just as you have the wonderful right to chase down your gifts, you must encourage the people around you to chase down their own gifts and help them in ways that meet their needs. You can regift in several different ways, depending on the person, their version of giftedness, and their current and near future interests. You can regift hard skills such as teaching a sport discipline or a work skill. You also can regift a life approach, such as how to act on a glimpse, endure, and transcend in the delivery of gifts by way of process. Through regifting, you are teaching another person the importance of sharing their gifts and supporting others into the future. Each of these options is a type of regifting, and each accomplishes an intended purpose.

Action Item Eight: Develop Your Regifting Game Plan

You encounter several people each day. You meet some people in your workplace, and some within your hobbies, social, and family life. As a first step, identify someone you have noticed to be trapped and struggling in the pursuit of one of their treasured gifts. Once you have identified the person, spend some deliberate time over the next three or four weeks and engage with this person to better understand how and why they are fenced in. The barrier might be their lack of life blend or asymmetry (discussed in lesson seven), because they feel too much of their time is devoted to one part of their life or one gift at the expense of other gifts that are being neglected.

For example, an exploratory gift led to the current planning exercise. I went out for a short run with a good friend several years ago while we were at a scientific meeting overseas. He is and has, for many years, been an accomplished athlete and successful marathoner. We were running on this beautiful street alongside a beach at dusk. Within seven or so minutes of the slow run and discussion, which was intended to help us unwind and restore our reserves, my friend's energy began to evaporate. The situation was to me almost identical to my story from several years earlier when I received my glimpse running alongside coaching staff at a sporting event where we were supporting national team athletes. My friend needed to pull up to a walk and came almost immediately to a standstill—he was nauseated and near the point of fainting. His face was pale to the point that it worried me. I waited with him and spoke reassuringly and without judgment. Within minutes, the discussion turned to self-neglect and prioritizing work life over good physical condition and taking care of personal well-being. The discussion continued at a nearby seaside restaurant over a cold drink, where my friend asked that we stay in touch regularly. My friend asked me to adopt the role of accountability partner. He requested that I follow up every few weeks and ask whether he was carving out time apart from work and family demands for runs and other forms of physical conditioning. My role in the regifting process had little to do with running and more to do with the soft skill of being supportive of this gifted but dormant athlete in a state of glimpsing the correction of a contorted path. He needed to begin immediate planning, preparation, and sustained action to return to a state of thriving—topics discussed in lessons four and five about glimpses and endurance.

Step one in this exercise of helping someone and regifting is to take the time to fully understand the imbalance or whatever barrier the person feels trapped by. Spend time with them, assuming you are a trusted colleague, friend, or family member, and help them explore how and why they are trapped in a state of contortion, just as I needed to do with my friend. Within these sorts of challenging discussions, explore whether their contortion is because colleagues are expecting too much of their time or whether the state of being trapped and contorted is of the person's own making. There might be more than one single reason why someone became trapped and contorted by competing forces. Your first step is to help them thoroughly explore where they are trapped to avoid premature solutions that might or might not align with the compromised person's long-term success. Premature solutions, as you know, never end in long-standing positive changes. My friend desired a premature solution to alleviate immediate discomfort without fully rooting out the problems, which is contrary to potential reevaluation and healthy change. Glimpses are important, but careful thought must be invested in how to repair a contorted state into one where the person is back on track and in symmetry, a topic considered in lesson seven. So, the first discussion you have must only be exploratory and an agreed upon beginning to more discussions to come.

For step two, once you both have a better understanding of where the barrier to better health or behavior is in relation to daily living, encourage your friend to map out a weekly plan in which a reblending of life, leading to a healthy shift, is inevitable but also realistic. If the issue is one of scheduling and competing priorities, have your friend or colleague pull out the weekly schedule presently being maintained. If the schedule is not fully written out, have your colleague write it out with as much detail as possible. Then, have the person self-evaluate whether it is as efficient as it needs to be to make space for a glimpse to be actioned. Are there redundancies and wasted time in the day that could be used better? Are there expectations for work productivity that belong in other hours and days within each week as compared with where they are currently placed? Step two requires your friend to reflect deeply on their current contortion. They might also reflect with a partner they are living with or an additional trusted friend who really understands their daily schedule. This process of reflection takes a week and requires some deep self-reflection on the part of your friend.

Step three is to meet with the person to consider potential refinements to their calendar and bring these to the follow-up discussion you are engaged in. Your job is to first listen to what your friend has learned and only then to serve as an objective adviser by suggesting possible schedule refinements, providing your friend is open to external feedback on their calendar of events. Together you can begin to refine the calendar and simplify any existing complexities or poorly placed activities that previously contributed to asymmetry and the inability to pursue their presently inaccessible gift. The discussion partway through step three is where you work together on the enhanced plan until your friend is fully satisfied and excited by the outcome from your shared exploratory discussion. This person must walk away from step three with a doable calendar in which the glimpsed gift can be integrated into the daily plan and become part of a healthy evolution and then a healthy habit. There will be initial foreseeable challenges to the necessary change. These challenges and their solutions should be identified in the discussion. Encourage your friend to keep track of these challenges over the following week and document them in terms of what the barrier was, how they responded, and whether the response was effective in terms of reinforcing the desired change. The meeting should conclude with a review of the action plan and a date for a third meeting.

Step four is where you become the accountability partner my friend requested as step one. As you know, it is one thing to develop an improved schedule to tap into a glimpsed gift, and another entirely to press a desired glimpse into action. Research relating to changes in behaviors has shown that embarking on a refined schedule and sticking with the new and improved life plan are entirely different challenges (80). One week after the person has acted and begun to regain symmetry through the addition of their gift, you must meet with the person, either in person or by video, so you can discuss it face-to-face. Your friend should review the week based on notes, provide some of the challenges and solutions, and share their status and any potential refinements that need to be made based on their change attempt. During this same meeting, you officially commit to becoming a longer-term accountability partner for at least a few months, until what was initially a new change in your friend or colleague becomes an established life pattern—one that is desired by its recipient. Keep in mind as you enter a few months of weekly follow-ups that the person you are supporting might need more than a follow-up call to stay on course. Often, the most desired task, even with the best of planning, can become a sizable barrier. One of the typical barriers I have heard over my time supporting friends is a runner not placing running shoes and that gorgeous running apparel by the door and taking it with them if they planned to start a run from somewhere other than their doorstep. If you are in physical proximity to your partner and have the time and interest, you could also commit to doing the activity together. I like to run, so for me it is easy to be a running buddy to a new runner or someone restarting. The important piece to this final step in your regifting exercise is for you to be patient with this other person. Remember, it is they who are making a considerable life change by integrating or reigniting a gift. You know from the lesson on endurance that they, just like you, will experience road bumps along the way. Do your best to encourage this person on their path and remember to reassure them that the journey includes potholes, but if they persevere, it will leave them satisfied and healthy with their giftedness.

⏰ Lesson Reminders

- ❖ Regifting is an important part of the gifting process. Just as we are supported in our gifts and have gained healthy lessons and benefits from the use of our gifts, we have an additional gift—that is, to regift skills or support to family, friends, and colleagues. This regifting is a necessary part of a healthy society because all people need their gifts supported and further developed.

- ❖ When you enter a regifting process, remember you are supporting someone else in their unique version of a gift. The gift might be a skill you are gifted with. However, every person must develop their gift based on who they are and use it in a way that benefits their path to giftedness. The tendency is often to attempt to teach the gift and expect others to use it just as you previously did or currently do. When regifting, ensure you are encouraging a creative use of the gift and not a cloned approach that duplicates your style.

- ❖ The regifting process is as beneficial to you as it is to the person being gifted. Gifts have life spans, such as the ability to compete in a sport or endure the physical demands of a workplace at the point in your career where you are operating at your most productive in terms of workload. There is a time to use your gift on the front lines, and there is an equally important time for you to share your experiences with the next generation. Sharing your gift allows you to continue with its use a different format. Think of the iconic boxer who became a boxing coach and mentor to his protégé. Both people's lives were enriched in the regifting process.

- ❖ You are someone with many opportunities to regift, and one of the most important pieces to sharing your knowledge and experience is to do so systematically. If you review the four-step process I proposed as an action item, what you will see is the need to regift step by step, no matter whether the person is in a state of crisis or is a potential candidate for regifting. If you follow a slow and steady strategy in this process, the person receiving your gift will benefit from your wisdom over the long term. The gift will be one that person will turn to and play with regularly. You, in turn, will have passed forward a gift that has served you well. Now, you can watch someone gain equal enjoyment from a passion you share.

CONCLUSION

Like you, I seek to live life to the fullest, more so now than ever before since writing this book and reflecting on the process of returning to my own personal gifts. Writing and reflecting, whether in a journal or in a book project such as this one, are growth exercises. The first words I penned were about my equine partner, Solitaire. Thinking about her continues to remind me of an important life lesson—uncharted freedom and the opportunity to bound over life's obstacles are necessary to cover more ground. Solitaire began this process long before I came along for the ride, and she did so without consent from others and despite their wishes for her to do otherwise. She then passed on her teaching to me, her partner and teammate. Like Solitaire, I move to my own drumbeat and map my own course in a continued harvest of gifts regardless of what others believe I should be doing. Life's path must be chosen by the person traveling the journey. The same message has now been passed to you. Make your choices and seize opportunities to grow and develop by refining existing gifts and discovering others not yet recognized, at least not consciously. Boundaries, convention, and inhibition are for the tamed and domesticated person, not for the adventurous spirit, the explorer, the evolving and engaged you!

Looking Forward

When you chose to read this book, you might not have known where your journey would take you. You might have glimpsed an opportunity, which then led you to read this book about giftedness. The reading process was crafted to help encourage you toward self-reflection in terms of where (and who) you need to be in your life, now and into the future. Life needs meaning. Some of that meaning comes from relationships. Relationships, especially with those who support your giftedness, are integral to the fulfillment of potential. Experience has taught you that you are most satisfied and at ease when you make decisions in favor of your giftedness. When you choose to tap into who you are and the amazing qualities that come naturally to you, you will always feel at inner peace. The benefits of tapping into your giftedness include happiness, stronger relationships, creativity, future-mindedness, and continued growth and are too many to list. The clichéd opposite to progression is life crisis caused by overlooking your gifts as time marches on. People who feel stalled out or boxed in cannot be happy; they will not thrive and risk passing on their poorly chosen life path to others of the same generation and the next generation. You are responsible to yourself and those you love to identify your gifts, commit to them, and chase them down. Continue to explore your giftedness from now until you cease to exist, and petition others to do the same.

In this book I have proposed eight lessons for you to follow in your growth process.

1. How to identify your gifts
2. How competing forces pull you toward and push you away from giftedness
3. How contortion occurs and what can be gained from it
4. How to recognize a personal glimpse and work with it to shape a better future
5. How to take positive action and endure in the pursuit of your gifts
6. How to develop a plan that leads to transcending in monumental uses of your gifts
7. How to become symmetrical in identifying, developing, and using gifts in a healthy blend
8. How to regift to others for their benefit and yours

The sequence of these lessons is unavoidable because one lesson must come before another when ideas are packaged into a book. Although you should read this book from beginning to end, you should return to the lessons you need most at a suitable time to be reminded of how to evolve with your gifts. If you forget about where you wish to go next, read the lesson about glimpses. If you are preparing to perform, revisit the lesson on transcendence. Life paths, which include the movement toward your gifts, cannot be linear. Your life will include complications that will pull you onto your path and crossroads where you will lose your way for a short time before you move forward once again toward your gifts. The distractions you experience are diversions, and from them you can learn life lessons that exist to strengthen your conviction to pursue your version of giftedness. Accept all setbacks that come your way; learn from them what needs to be learned; then endure, transcend, and strive for symmetry.

These reflections are built from the different gifts I draw on in my own life. I have aligned my values and actions using the same processes woven throughout these eight lessons. The content has been inspired by my personal experience as a former elite athlete, especially where my earlier athletic career permitted me to travel afterward in the applications of old gifts and the discovery of new gifts. The content was influenced by the world of high-performance sports, where people train to perform each day and work on their fine edge toward excellence. The stories and examples came from discussions and life lived on the road with high-performance athletes, their working staff, and management. Although first-hand experiences were central to the curating of the lessons, so too was the scientific research I have read, developed, and field tested with amateur and professional athletes. Sports, the driving force in this book, is an elite performance environment, much like the elite environments of business, law, engineering, education, or the fine arts. The context you live in parallels the world of sports; so the lessons inspired by sports are transferable to your improved life path. You are a performer, and you are being asked to perform as you!

Just as you have been on a reflective process, a quest to draw upon your gifts, I embarked on a quest of my own. I wrote this book during a fascinating year that held many opportunities to tap into and expand upon my own version of giftedness. The world had come to a standstill during the pandemic, each day colored by the push and pull of advancement and loss. Advancements in science were taking place amid the Herculean effort of combating COVID-19 with a vaccine and other public health measures, the loss of human contact, and the ultimate loss of millions of lives.

I began to write this book in late winter of a new year, just as the last snowflakes were falling and the sun began warming my bones. Hope was on the horizon, case numbers were declining, and people were emerging from their respective lockdowns with the newness of a spring flower. The conceptualizing and writing process were entirely before me. I was excited and yet fearful of the immense thought and energy needed to crystallize ideas about giftedness into words. How might they be presented, sequenced, and unpacked in a way that made sense? I pondered on giftedness and how people, including me, contort to meet life's demands.

Then early spring arrived, and I continued to write while I turned my attention to the final months of preparation for the Tokyo Olympics, until then, an uncertain event for the athletes (81). These same athletes wrestled with the competing forces of preparing to be an Olympian competitor without the assurance that the Olympics would be held (82). By the middle of spring, I was helping to prepare the athletes for travel once more to a global tournament, this time one of the most visible sporting events on the world stage. The transition back to competition and advancement opportunities was jolting because it followed a period when many athletes had been unable to compete. While working with the athletes who successfully qualified, I began writing the lesson about endurance, all the while thinking about how to retain the interest of athletes who would have to wait for the next global sports event because of the unforeseen lack of access to qualification events. Indeed, many athletes could have qualified, some who were relative newcomers, yet there were no final qualification events within reach.

When early summer arrived and it was almost time for the Olympics to begin, I packed my gear, hugged my wife and children goodbye, boarded my first postpandemic plane, and headed to a pre-Olympic training camp where the athletes and coaches were embarking on final preparation and fine-tuning. During that training camp I wrote about transcendence. While in Tokyo, I continued to invest in this book, with my attention placed on finalizing thoughts about transcendence, just as the athletes were seeking to play out its meaning in one part of their lives. I polished prose and ordered paragraphs until they represented my deepest-rooted beliefs and sequencing about human gifts and how these need to germinate over time until they sprout plants and eventually bear fruit. The flight home consisted of hours of continued engagement as I reflected on the challenges and triumphs I witnessed and supported on-site. I sat beside athletes, parents, and coaches in shared laughter as the second-to-last lesson for this book was being thought through. I watched, listened, reflected, and wrote some more, this time as I launched into what symmetry represents and how it can be integrated into a discussion about the extraordinariness of gifts. In late summer, I reengaged with my family and restored symmetry in my own life.

Throughout reassimilation, I continued to consider what others might be doing—lamenting the loss felt of having completed Olympics (asymmetry caused by a singular, yet profound application of their gifts) without sufficient optimism for what was to come next, perhaps something different but equally monumental. My family and I explored national parks, visited friends, and just played as I continued to contemplate this book project, its written words, and their potential uptake.

Then another special moment arrived as I was refining this book and searching for a literary agent. I had been training all spring, summer, and early fall to compete in running. I entered and ran an international virtual half marathon, one I had always wanted to participate in: the Toronto Waterfront Half Marathon. I woke up early on the chosen morning and steeled myself to endure the surges and strains of running 21.1 kilometers (13.1 miles) on my own, physically isolated from competitors. The first 10 miles went extremely well, and I was truly the best version of my master's running self. Then I began to struggle with fatigue almost out of nowhere. By living out the words I had spent many months writing, words from giftedness through transcendence in my own mind and body, I dug deep and won my age group. I was among the top 20 of more than 1,200 total finishers. Time during the run, much as in the writing of this book, was my friend—relished, listened to, and even dialogued with. Within the same autumn university term, I returned to class and worked with enthused graduate students, my own protégés, helping them find their own path. I was reminded just how much I love to regift and see others flourish, not only as aspiring professionals but also as fit, healthy, and symmetrical people.

Within the activity of writing, I was once more performing to my fullest in many different, equally exciting moments. I, like you, have and will continue to be fully committed to living out gifts across different fields—some past, some current, others in preparation, and still others yet to be charted, awaiting future glimpses. We may look at the world around us and recognize many colleagues, friends, and acquaintances who feel they are trapped in an unsatisfying life of their own making. People who at one time believed they could chart their own path and then push themselves to uncharted areas but instead relinquished themselves to a much slower, confined, and predictable life. Many people speak about retirement as if it will provide the opportunity to once more tap into their passions and giftedness. Some will wait eagerly for days to pass in the belief that in the future they will be able to live unbounded again. However, a promise to alter yourself in the future does not result in playing out your full potential. Unlike the delivery of fast food, gifts need to be developed and curated so they can be practiced in many different parts of each day. No one else can lead our collective evolution, although our loved ones hope we continue to materialize and remain engaged with the world around us. How are you to do so if you are not authentically drawing upon your gifts? If you have read to the very end of this book, you are a seeker, someone who is always looking forward while appreciating the past. We each have a past, a present, and a future. Each time in your life is an opportune time to maximize potential, but your glimpses must turn to concrete actions, just as seeds in a garden must be planted, watered, nourished, and tended, leading to the next season of growth.

A Parting Gift

Now to a final request. Throughout this book you have read stories shared from key transitional moments in my life. Each of the stories reflects a growth period, ones that pushed me forward to the next exciting application of my gifts—from young athlete to world-cup competitor, to graduate student, to young professional, to international practitioner, to seasoned educator working with the next generation of learners. You have an equivalent opportunity to put pen to paper. Think back to the first time you remember engaging with your gifts. The experience might have been in sports, dance, writing, debating, or another context altogether. Dare to write about your own first experience with your giftedness. Explore it and craft your story with vibrancy and emotion. You will know when you have crafted the story as it is meant to be, as your initial encounter with greatness. Reading the story will stir your emotions, just as reading my first story about my equine partner has done, time and again, for me.

Next, take the time and identify the next stage in your life where you intentionally or accidentally applied your gift. Gifts always resurface at opportune and inopportune moments. Take the time to think about the second monumental application of your gifts, how these were tapped and why. Build the second story as meaningfully as the first. Continue to write these stories until you have at least five. To draw inspiration for these stories, of course, circle back to the ones I wrote from my different moments of development. Once you have completed your writing and the momentary reflections that came with each, consider your evolution. What you will find is each story of greatness, even if it came after several detours, reflects a truth: Your gifts are alive, they resurface, and when they do, the moments need to be recognized and treasured. Your mission going forward is to continue and weave together stories to reveal and encourage your evolution as you continue to forge your path. You have gifts well suited for each life stage as opposed to gifts confined to one moment in time. You have a past, a present, and a future, all demanding only the very best of you. I wish you a continued quest and discovery of your giftedness. It is your birthright!

GLOSSARY

action—Moving from a state of thinking and planning to a state of doing. When this step is taken before a structure is put in place to sustain the action, you will likely falter and discontinue in a gift pursuit. When planning is well developed, action is easier to maintain, leading to endurance and a better-developed gift.

affirmations—Statements that reinforce your objectives, written in past tense as "I am" statements. Affirmations should be written so that they are specific, measurable, attainable, relevant, and time-based.

artifacts—Daily visual reminders used to keep you on track and inspired. Examples might include an inspiring image of your dream gift being lived out, qualifications for a position or designation, a competition poster, and any other significant item you can place in your home and work environment to keep you on your path toward giftedness.

authentic—Your most sincere and honest behaviors and choices, which are emphasized throughout this book in place of a version of self that does not fully capture your giftedness. If you apply your gifts and pursue your interests in a way that is true to yourself, you are on the path you are meant to live, drawing on the correct forces. There is a sense of well-being when you are authentically you.

birthright—The way you are meant to carry out life based on your predispositions and innate gifts. Each person, you included, has a birthright to draw on their inherited gifts, but not all people choose to recognize or take advantage of these personal qualities. The intention is to spend as much of each day as possible in an environment where you can act upon your gifts.

contortions—Discordance caused by subduing a gift, choosing not to use it, or hiding it for a prolonged time, such as when you deviate from the pursuit of acting, musical talents, kind behaviors, educational pursuits, or sports dreams. The contorted person becomes someone other than who they know themselves to be by nature because of influences harmful to their personal development. Internal and external influences contribute to contortion when we permit these influences to rule our actions. Contortion will eventually lead to sadness and compromised mental health in place of thriving.

debriefing—A strategy you can use to make sense of your performances. This strategy compels you to examine personal accountability and look beyond when the misstep happened to the reasons of why and how it happened. Debriefing also includes identifying healthy decisions and strategies during a recent performance so that you can reintegrate these systematically in the future. This process is challenging because it necessitates time investment on your part after each important performance, so that learning leads to improved actions and more giftedness.

disputing—Challenging any negative thinking that is getting in the way of high-level performance. This skill is used to challenge the accuracy of an unfolding negative possibility and then downsizes negative anticipation until it is proportionately one that can be overcome, clearing the path toward positive action and the manifestation of your gifts. Negative thoughts are opposed and dispelled using positive previous experiences and rational thinking that tie in one's personal skills and any useful strategies to move you forward in each gift pursuit.

endurance—Investing regular hours each day in yourself, without fail, despite challenges. Endurance reveals a willingness and desire to persist in your gift from one day to the next over months so that they become an integral part of you. The best world-class performers are relentless in their endurance toward their goals. However, many people choose not to endure in the pursuit of their gifts.

forces—The energy pulling you toward and away from your gifts. A positive force pulls you magnetically toward your gift, such as when you decide to prioritize the gift over a competing work or social demand that would otherwise deter you. A negative force is one that repels your dreams and prevails when you choose to act in a way that postpones the use of your gifts, such as when you choose to do a mundane task in a conventional way and, in the process, opt not to draw upon skills that bring out your potential.

fundamental attribution errors—The tendency within every person to explain other peoples' behaviors, when these are misguided, to their disposition while ascribing personal behaviors, especially after a setback, to the situation and not to oneself. This pattern slows self-reflection and learning about how to improve personal performance while sometimes not being as forgiving as we should toward the actions of people around us who can support us in our quests for excellence and giftedness.

gifts—Personal characteristics or qualities that are your natural inclinations, comparatively well above average to the norm, and unique to you. Talents, such as being musical, are gifts, but the term *gift* also extends to parts of a person's thinking or disposition, including the tendency to be relentless and persistent when others often are not. Gifts are plentiful in each person, but only sometimes do they manifest into reality when they are deliberately pursued.

glimpses—A "sixth sense" you have when future possibilities surface or resurface in the mind's eye and are felt as a bodily sensation. They are typically brief and experienced as a fleeting reminder of a gift possibility; often, however, they are not acted upon as you move through your days. You must remain open to glimpses when these are experienced, recognize them, and then contemplate the timing of the gift in relation to action. The alternate pathways to ignoring your gifts will lead to inauthentic actions.

imagery—The mental strategy of playing out an optimal performance using your human senses, such as visual cues, sound, taste, and touch. This mental skill is used by performers to think through the application of their gifts in different performance environments, where optimal responses can be seen and felt through a meditative process. Imagery also can serve to inspire the performer in you when its application is focused on achieving a successful outcome and experiencing its rewards.

lessons—Important parts of an ever-improving gifting process that can be developed in a sequence but must be visited and revisited when most needed to strengthen a gift.

mental performance consultant—A professional with a background in psychology, sport science, or an allied helping profession, who is trained to reinforce personal mental skills in the performance domain and share the application of theoretical frameworks and practical exercises used to help instill, maintain, and further motivate toward one's gifts.

mental skills—A series of motivational exercises that are used, much like a carpenter's tools, to build motivation and giftedness. There are several skills that you must practice and refine over time to strengthen and then act upon your gifts through performance. These skills include but are not limited to imagery (multisensory visualization), goal setting, planning, relaxation, arousal, concentration, and debriefing. No two people will use a given mental skill the same way, so there is always uniqueness in terms of how they are applied by you.

path—The pursuit of a journey toward a gift that you have identified. Your chosen path will include the movement toward and away from your gifts throughout a life course. When you are on your best-suited, most authentic path, you will feel a high degree of harmony and positive thoughts and emotions, because you are acting upon who you are meant to be by design.

planning—A reciprocal process built from previous debriefing lessons gained from earlier performances that considers food, hydration, sleep, support from others, thinking patterns, tactical decisions, and more, as parts of a step-by-step performance strategy to move you, the gifted performer, from practice and simulation toward and through each transcendent performance. The planning process is unique to each person based on your best practices, which differs to some extent from anyone else's.

reflect—Your inward examination of thoughts and feelings that enables you to learn and evolve toward your gifts. People engaging in a reflective process might do so alone but could benefit from a supportive friend or partner in the quest to learn more about how to tap into personal potential. Reflection can be achieved by examining your experience, considering your accountability, identifying your strengths and weaknesses, and then integrating lessons from the evaluation process into your daily life from that point onward. The opposite to reflection is a continued pattern without the recognition of necessary lessons to build deeper knowledge and improved performance.

regifting—When you support another person's gifts to counterbalance the support previously experienced by you when you were being nourished in the pursuit of personal gifts. Passing on one's gifts or supporting the gifts of another person creates healthier workplaces and personal lives as people within the surrounding environment are also able to share in the experience of thriving and its formation in a wider network of family, friends, and peers.

resourceful—Tapping into best-suited potential and supplemental support from friends, family, colleagues, and experts within one's reach. A person who undertakes this response differs from one who is reliant on a few skills or people, which might not be the only necessary resources to support one's gifts in application. The intention is to develop a strong repertoire of your resources and choose what best fits in relation to the challenge you are undertaking.

simulation—A sequence of dress rehearsal strategies in advance of your transcendent performance. This systematic process begins with a simple walk through of the performance, where the gift is to eventually be used under pressure. The simulation process is developed systematically to sequentially include uncomplicated first attempts, followed by scenarios with potential distractions and more challenging opposition to one's gifts. Simulations are an important precursor to extraordinary performance, because people need to apply their gifts in various circumstances before applying them with conviction in the heat of the monumental performance, such as an elite sports event or sought-after life dream where one lives out their gifts.

stories—Fictional or nonfictional accounts used to capture an idea, or in the case of this book, an important developmental step in the form of a personal gift. Every person, including you, has garnered stories from their life history. These stories should be used to mark how a gift is played out to its fullest and as a reminder of your past, which happens to be a foundation to your future pursuits and the living out of your next gift.

symmetry—A balanced approach to life where the most prized parts of yourself are integrated into each day. The term signifies a holistic approach to the application of your gifts in personal life, play, and work, as opposed to an unbalanced existence where a gift is only applied in one part of your daily living, meaning you are experiencing asymmetry in your day. Unlike the person in symmetry, an asymmetrical life, accumulated through unbalanced days, leads to life imbalance, unhappiness, and your inability to live out each strength to its fullest.

thriving—A state in which you are living at your optimal level. People in a state of thriving excel in many parts of their life. You will know you are in a state of thriving because you will have a sunny disposition and high level of daily energy. You will also be patient and forgiving with others nearby. States of thriving are contrasted with times when you are not satisfied with your current state of being. You will sense inertia and frustration in terms of the application of your gifts. These unsettling states are meant to remind you that changes are needed to restore a thriving existence.

transcendence—The performance of your gifts at an elevated level previously not achieved, meaning your performance is unparalleled. The term signifies a progressive step in the use of your human gifts where you discover and create heightened capacity. So long as you are in pursuit of a gift, you should always seek to transcend previous performance levels by seeking out new opportunities and by pushing your boundaries of just how far you can push a gift's limits.

REFERENCES

1. Association for Applied Sport Psychology. (n.d.). *Certification*. https://appliedsportpsych.org/certification/
2. Schinke, R.J., & Hackfort, D. (Eds.). (2017). *Psychology in professional sport and the performing arts: Competencies, approaches, and interventions*. Routledge.
3. Orlick. T. (2016). *In pursuit of excellence* (5th ed.). Human Kinetics.
4. Seligman, M.E.P. (2006). *Learned optimism: How to change your mind and your life*. Vintage Books.
5. Martens, R. (1987). Science, knowledge, and sport psychology. *The Sport Psychologist, 1*(1), 29-55.
6. Seligman, M.E.P., Steen, T.A., Park, N., & Peterson, C. (2005). Positive psychology progress: Empirical validation of interventions. *American Psychologist, 60*(5), 410-421.
7. Fletcher, D., & Sarkar, M. (2012). A grounded theory of psychological resilience in Olympic champions. *Psychology of Sport and Exercise, 13*(5), 669-678.
8. Schinke, R.J., da Costa, J., & Andrews, M. (2001). Social cognitive considerations regarding graduate student difficulties. *Alberta Journal of Education, 47*(4), 342-353.
9. Dube, T.V., Schinke, R.J., Strasser, R., & Couper, I. (2016). Adaptation to transition during clinical clerkship: What is known about the medical student's perspective? *Medical Education, 49*(10), 1028-1037.
10. TheNHLhistory. *Legends of hockey: Phil Esposito* [Video]. YouTube. www.youtube.com/watch?v=391-Blebyuo.
11. International Society of Sport Psychology. *Leadership*. https://issponline.org/about/leadership/
12. Bonhomme, J., Schinke, R.J., Blodgett, A.T., & Stambulova, N. (2020). The career trajectories of two world champion boxers: Interpretive thematic analysis of media data. *Sport in Society, 23*(4), 560-576.
13. Schinke, R.J., Stambulova, N.B., Trepanier, D., & Oghene, P. (2015). Psychological support for the Canadian Olympic Boxing Team in meta-transitions through the National Team Program.

International Journal of Sport and Exercise Psychology, 13(1), 74-89.

14. Battochio, R.C., Schinke, R.J., & Stambulova, N. (2019). Barriers in the careers of National Hockey League players. *International Journal of Sport Psychology, 50*(5), 448-468.

15. Locke, E.A., & Latham, G.P. (2002). Building a practically useful theory of goal setting and task motivation: A 35-year odyssey. *American Psychologist, 57*(9), 705-717.

16. Schinke, R.J., Jerome, W., & Couture, R. (2005). Social support and national team athletes with different perceptions. *Avante, 11*(1), 56-66.

17. Stiroh, K.J. (2007). Playing for keeps: Pay and performance in the NBA. *Economic Inquiry, 45*(1), 145-161.

18. Schinke, R.J. (2000). *Major games competence development*. [Unpublished doctoral dissertation]. University of Alberta.

19. Luginbuhl, J., & Bell, A. (1989). Causal attributions by athletes: Role of ego involvement. *Journal of Sport and Exercise Psychology, 11*(4), 399-407.

20. Weston, N.J., Greenlees, I.A., & Thelwell, R.C. (2011). Athlete perceptions of the impacts of performance profiling. *International Journal of Sport and Exercise Psychology, 9*(2), 173-188.

21. Weiser, M., & Garibaldi, G. (2015). Quantifying motivational deficits and apathy: A review of literature. *European Neuropsychopharmacology, 25*(8), 1060-1081.

22. Industry Canada. (2011, January 20). *Government of Canada celebrates three new Canada Research Chairs at Laurentian University*. www.globenewswire.com/news-release/2011/01/20/1403732/0/en/Government-of-Canada-Celebrates-Three-New-Canada-Research-Chairs-at-Laurentian-University.html

23. NHL. *Wayne Gretzky all time leader in goals, points* [Video.] YouTube. www.youtube.com/watch?v=tlY7sL8qP8U

24. NHL. *Mark Messier was one of NHL's greatest leaders* [Video.] YouTube. www.youtube.com/watch?v=KI4lDBwYF5U

25. Watzlawick, P. (1993). *The situation is hopeless, but not serious (The pursuit of unhappiness)*. W.W. Norton & Company.

26. McArdle, S., Martin, D., Lennon, A., & Moore, P. (2010). Exploring debriefing in sports: A qualitative perspective. *Journal of Applied Sport Psychology, 22*(3), 320-332.

27. Schinke, R.J., & da Costa, J. (2001). Understanding the development of major-games competitors' explanations and behaviors

from a contextual viewpoint. *Athletic Insight, 3*(3), Retrieved December 21, 2023, from https://www.athleticinsight.com/Vol3Iss3/ExplanationPDF.pdf
28. Ratner, B. (Director). (2000). *The family man* [Film]. Universal.
29. Grusec, J.E. (1994). Social learning theory and developmental psychology: The legacies of Robert R. Sears and Albert Bandura. In R.D. Parke, P.A. Ornstein, J.J. Rieser, & C. Zahn-Waxler (Eds.), *A century of developmental psychology* (pp. 473-497). American Psychological Association.
30. Schinke, R.J., & Stambulova, N. (2017). Context-driven sport and exercise psychology practice: Widening our lens beyond the athlete. *Journal of Sport Psychology in Action, 8*(2), 71-75.
31. Prochaska, J.O., Redding, C.A., & Evers, K.E. (2015). The transtheoretical model and stages of change. In K. Glanz, B.K. Rimer, & K. Biswanath (Eds.), *Health behavior: Theory, research, and practice* (pp. 125-148). Jossey-Bass.
32. Rollnick, S., Butler, C.C., Kinnersley, P., Gregory, J., & Mash, B. (2010). Motivational interviewing. *BMJ, 340*, c1900. https://doi.org/10.1136/bmj.c1900
33. Gardner, B. (2015). A review and analysis of the use of "habit" in understanding, predicting, and influencing health-related behavior. *Health Psychology Review, 9*(3), 277-295.
34. Blodgett, A.T., Coholic, D., Schinke, R.J., McGannon, K.R., Peltier, D., & Pheasant, C. (2013). Moving beyond words: Exploring the use of an arts-based method in Aboriginal community sport research. *Qualitative Research in Sport, Exercise and Health, 5*(3), 312-331.
35. Schinke, R.J., Blodgett. A.T., Kao, S.F., & Ryba, T.V. (2019). Cultural sport psychology as a pathway to advances in identity and settlement research to practice. *Psychology of Sport and Exercise, 42*, 58-65.
36. Peters, H.J., & Williams, J.M. (2006). Moving cultural background to the foreground: An investigation of self-talk, performance, and persistence following feedback. *Journal of Applied Sport Psychology, 18*(3), 240-253.
37. Orlick, T., & Partington, J. (1986). *Psyched: Inner views of winning*. Coaching Association of Canada.
38. Ade, D., Seifert, L., Gal-Petitfaux, N., & Poizat, G. (2017). Artefacts and expertise in sport: An empirical study of ice climbing. *International Journal of Sport Psychology, 48*(1), 82-98.

39. Cohen, G.L., & Sherman, D. (2014). The psychology of change: Self-affirmation and social psychological intervention. *Annual Review of Psychology, 65*, 333-371.
40. Hutchinson, A. (2018). *Endure*. Harper Collins.
41. Lally, P., van Jaarsveld, C.H.M., Potts, H.W.W., & Wardle, J. (2010). How are habits formed: Modelling habit formation in the real world. *European Journal of Social Psychology, 40*(6), 998-1009.
42. Maddux, J.E. (1997). Habit, health, and happiness. *Journal of Sport & Exercise Psychology, 19*(4), 331-346.
43. Howells, K., Sarkar, M., & Fletcher, D. (2017). Can athletes benefit from adversity? A systematic review of growth following adversity in competitive sport. *Progress in Brain Research, 234*, 117-159.
44. Hogg, J.M. (1998). The post-performance debriefing process: Getting your capable track and field athletes to the next level of performance. *New Studies in Athletics, 13*(3), 49-56.
45. Schinke, R.J. (2010). *The mental edge in boxing*. Nova Science Publishers.
46. Schinke, R.J., Tenenbaum, G., Lidor, R., & Battochio, R.C. (2010). Adaptation in action: The transition from research to intervention. *The Sport Psychologist, 24*(4), 542-557.
47. Galli, N., & Vealey, R.S. (2008). "Bouncing back" from adversity: Athletes' experiences of resilience. *The Sport Psychologist, 22*(3), 316-335.
48. Harvey, J.H., Town, J.P., & Yarkin, K.L. (1981). How fundamental is "the fundamental attribution error"? *Journal of Personality and Social Psychology, 40*(2), 346-349.
49. Ellis, A. (2008). Cognitive restructuring of the disputing of irrational beliefs. In W.T. O'Donohue & J.E. Fisher (Eds.), *Cognitive behavior therapy: Applying empirically supported techniques in your practice* (pp. 91-95). John Wiley & Sons.
50. Maier, S.F., & Seligman, M.E.P. (2016). Learned helplessness at fifty: Insights from neuroscience. *Psychological Review, 123*(4), 349-367.
51. Sheridan, D., Coffee, P., & Lavallee, D. (2014). A systematic review of social support in youth sport. *International Review of Sport and Exercise Psychology, 7*(1), 198-228.
52. Neil, R., Hanton, S., & Mellalieu, S.D. (2013). Seeing things in a different light: Assessing the effects of a cognitive-behavioral

intervention upon the further appraisals of golfers. *Journal of Applied Sport Psychology, 25*(1), 106-130.

53. Sammy, N., Anstiss, P.A., Moore, L.J., Freeman, P., Wilson, M.R., & Vine, S.J. (2017). The effects of arousal reappraisal on stress responses, performance, and attention. *Anxiety, Stress and Coping, 30*(6), 619-629.

54. Mann, M. (Director). (2001). *Ali*. [Film]. Columbia.

55. Schinke, R.J. (2012). *The champion in you: Lessons learned from professional boxing about how to succeed in life and work*. Nova Science Publishers.

56. Anderson, R., Hanrahan, S.J., & Mallett, C.J. (2014). Investigating the optimal psychological state for peak performance in Australian elite athletes. *Journal of Applied Sport Psychology, 26*(3), 318-333.

57. Jackson, S.A. (1996). Toward a conceptual understanding of the flow experience in elite athletes. *Research Quarterly for Exercise and Sport, 67*(1), 76-90.

58. Schinke, R.J., Peterson, C., & Couture, R. (2004). A protocol for teaching resilience to national team athletes. *Journal of Excellence, 8*(4), 9-18.

59. Schinke, R.J., Stambulova, N., Si, G., & Moore, Z. (2018). International Society of Sport Psychology position stand: Athletes' mental health, performance, and development. *International Journal of Sport and Exercise Psychology, 16*(6), 622-639.

60. Shatté, A., Gillham, J., & Reivich, K.J. (2000). Promoting hope in children and Adolescents. In J. Gillham (Ed.), *The science of optimism and hope: Research essays in honor of Martin E. P. Seligman* (pp. 215-234). Temple Press.

61. Schinke, R.J. (2016). Longstanding consultancy with elite professional boxers and their working teams. In R.J. Schinke, & D. Hackfort (Eds.), *The Routledge companion of professional sport and performance psychology* (pp. 127-139). Routledge.

62. Jackson, S.A., Dover, J., & Mayocchi, L. (1998). Life after winning gold: Experiences of Australian Olympic gold medalists. *The Sport Psychologist, 12*(2), 119-136.

63. Li, Y., Schinke, R.J., Middleton, T.R.F., Li, P., Si, G., & Zhang, L. (2023). The contextualization of Chinese athletes' careers in the Chinese whole nation system. *International Journal of Sport and Exercise Psychology, 21*(1), 138-155.

64. Werthner, P., & Orlick, T. (1986). Retirement experiences of successful Olympic athletes. *International Journal of Sport Psychology, 17*(5), 337-363.
65. Sinclair, D., & Orlick, T. (1993). Positive transitions from high-performance sport. *The Sport Psychologist, 7*(2), 138-150.
66. Stambulova, N.B. (2016). Athletes' transitions in sport and life: Positioning new research trends within existing system of athlete career knowledge. In R.J. Schinke, K. McGannon, & B. Smith (Eds.), *The Routledge international handbook of sport psychology* (pp. 519-535). Routledge.
67. Russo, M., Shteigman, A., & Carmelia, A. (2016). Workplace and family support and work-life balance: Implications for individual psychological availability and energy at work. *The Journal of Positive Psychology, 11*(2), 173-188.
68. Schinke, R.J., & McGannon, K.R. (2015). Cultural sport psychology and intersecting identities: An introduction to the special section. *Psychology of Sport and Exercise, 17*, 45-47.
69. Nicholls, A.R., Polman, R., & Levy, A.R. (2010). Coping self-efficacy, pre-competitive anxiety, and subjective performance among athletes. *European Journal of Sport Science, 10*(2), 97-102.
70. Blodgett, A.T., Ge, Y., Schinke, R.J., & McGannon. K.R. (2017). Intersecting identities of elite female boxers: Stories of cultural difference and marginalization in sport. *Psychology of Sport and Exercise, 32*, 83-92.
71. Henriksen, K., Schinke, R.J., Moesch, K., McCann, S., Parham, W., Terry, P., & Larsen, C. (2019). Consensus statement on improving the mental health of high-performance athletes. *International Journal of Sport and Exercise Psychology, 18*(5), 391-408.
72. Knights, S., Sherry, E., & Ruddock-Hudson, M. (2016). Investigating elite end-of-athletic-career transition: A systematic review. *Journal of Applied Sport Psychology, 28*(3), 291-308.
73. Schinke, R.J., Ge, Y., Blodgett, A.T., Petersen, B., Dupuis-Latour, J., & Coholic, D. (2019). Building a national team context based upon the identity challenges and intervention strategies of elite female boxers in their home environment. *Journal of Sport Psychology in Action, 10*(2), 94-105.
74. Meeusen, R., Duclos, M., Foster, C., Fry, A., Gleeson, M., Nieman, D., Raglin, J., Rietjens, G., Steinacker, J., & Urhausen, A. (2013). Prevention, diagnosis, and treatment of the overtraining syndrome: Joint consensus statement of the European College

of sport science (ECSS) and the American College of sports medicine (ACSM). *European Journal of Sport Science, 13*(1), 1-24.

75. Moesch, K., Kenttä, G., Kleinert, J., Quignon-Fleuret, C., Cecil, S., & Bertollo, M. (2018). FEPSAC position statement: Mental health disorders in elite athletes and models of service provision. *Psychology of Sport and Exercise, 38*, 61-71.

76. Henriksen, K., Schinke, R.J., McCann, S., Durand-Bush, N., Moesch, K., Parham, W.D., Larsen, C.H., Cogan, K., Donaldson, A., Poczwardowski, A., Noce, F., & Hunziker, J. (2020). Athlete mental health in the Olympic cycle: A consensus statement. *International Journal of Sport and Exercise Psychology, 18*(3), 553-560.

77. Bandura, A. (1997). *Self-efficacy: The exercise of control.* W.H. Freeman/Times Books/Henry Holt & Co.

78. Erickson, K., Bruner, M.W., MacDonald, D.J., & Cote, J. (2008). Gaining insight into actual and preferred sources of coaching knowledge. *International Journal of Sport Science and Coaching, 3*(4), 527-538.

79. Bandura, A. (1990). Perceived self-efficacy in the exercise of personal agency. *Journal of Applied Sport Psychology, 2*(2), 128-163.

80. De Brujin, G.J., & Rhodes, R.E. (2011). Exploring exercise behavior, intention, and habit strength relationships. *Scandinavian Journal of Medicine & Science in Sports, 21*(3), 482-491.

81. Schinke, R.J., Papaioannou, A., Henriksen, K., Si, G., Zhang, L., & Haberl, P. (2020). Sport psychology services to high-performance athletes during COVID-19. *International Journal of Sport and Exercise Psychology, 18*(3), 269-272.

82. Stambulova, N.B., Schinke, R.J., Lavallee, D., & Wylleman, P. (2022). The COVID-19 Pandemic and Olympic/Paralympic athletes' developmental challenges and possibilities in times of a global crisis-transition. *International Journal of Sport and Exercise Psychology, 20*(1), 92-101.

ABOUT THE AUTHOR

Robert J. Schinke, EdD, is a professor of kinesiology and health sciences at Laurentian University in Sudbury, Ontario, Canada. He is a distinguished professor in several high-profile international universities and a Canada Research Chair. He serves as senior coeditor for the *International Journal of Sport and Exercise Psychology* and editor in chief of the *Journal of Sport Psychology in Action*. His research has been profiled by leading national and international granting agencies, including the International Olympic Committee's Advanced Olympic Research Program, and his scientific publications have spanned more than 200 works on the topics of mental health, identity, inclusiveness, life transitions, and context-driven practice. Schinke currently serves as president of the International Society of Sport Psychology (ISSP). He previously served as president of the Association for Applied Sport Psychology (AASP), and he is a fellow of various sport and exercise psychology societies. Since 2000, Schinke has worked extensively with world-champion professional athletes as well as athletes at several Olympic Games. His work and ideas have been featured in *USA Today*, *The Globe and Mail*, Al Jazeera, HBO, and Showtime, among many other media outlets.

Find more outstanding resources at

US.HumanKinetics.com
Canada.HumanKinetics.com

In the **U.S.** call 1-800-747-4457
Canada 1-800-465-7301
International 1-217-351-5076

HUMAN KINETICS

Sign up for our newsletters!
Get the latest insights with regular newsletters, plus periodic product information and special insider offers from Human Kinetics.